Bond
No.1 for exam success

Non-verbal Reasoning

Assessment Papers

Challenge

10–11+ years

OXFORD
UNIVERSITY PRESS

OXFORD
UNIVERSITY PRESS

Great Clarendon Street, Oxford, OX2 6DP, United Kingdom

Oxford University Press is a department of the University of Oxford.
It furthers the University's objective of excellence in research,
scholarship, and education by publishing worldwide.

Oxford is a registered trade mark of Oxford University Press
in the UK and in certain other countries

Text © Alison Primrose 2015
Illustrations © Oxford University Press 2015

The moral rights of the authors have been asserted

First published in 2015
This edition published in 2021

All rights reserved. No part of this publication may be reproduced,
stored in a retrieval system, or transmitted, in any form or by any
means, without the prior permission in writing of Oxford University
Press, or as expressly permitted by law, by licence or under terms
agreed with the appropriate reprographics rights organization.
Enquiries concerning reproduction outside the scope of the above
should be sent to the Rights Department, Oxford University Press,
at the address above.

You must not circulate this work in any other form and you must
impose this same condition on any acquirer

British Library Cataloguing in Publication Data

Data available

978-0-19-277831-4

10 9 8 7 6 5 4 3 2 1

Paper used in the production of this book is a natural, recyclable
product made from wood grown in sustainable forests.

The manufacturing process conforms to the environmental
regulations of the country of origin.

Printed in China

Acknowledgements

The publishers would like to thank the following for permissions
to use copyright material:

Page make-up: eMC Design Ltd
Illustrations: Peters & Zabransky
Cover illustrations: Lo Cole

Although we have made every effort to trace and contact all
copyright holders before publication this has not been possible
in all cases. If notified, the publisher will rectify any errors or
omissions at the earliest opportunity.

Links to third party websites are provided by Oxford in good faith
and for information only. Oxford disclaims any responsibility for
the materials contained in any third party website referenced
in this work.

Introduction

The Bond *Challenge* titles are the most stretching of the Bond assessment papers, the number one series for the 11+, selective exams and general practice. Bond *Challenge* is carefully designed to stretch above and beyond the level provided in the regular Bond assessment range.

How does this book work?

The book contains two distinct sets of papers, along with fully explained answers and a progress chart:

- Focus tests, accompanied by advice and directions, which are focused on particular (and age-appropriate) Non-verbal Reasoning question types encountered in the 11+ and other exams, but devised at a higher level than the standard Assessment papers. Each focus test is designed to help raise a child's skills in the question type, as well as offer plenty of practice for the necessary techniques.
- Mixed papers, which are full-length tests containing a full range of Non-verbal Reasoning question types. These are designed to provide rigorous practice, perhaps against the clock, for children working at a level higher than that required to pass at the 11+ and other Non-verbal Reasoning tests.
- Fully explained answers are provided for both types of test in the middle of the book.
- At the back of the book, there is a progress chart which allows you to track your child's progress. In the Mixed papers we have aligned question types with numbers, so you can identify where your child is performing well or struggling.

How much time should the tests take?

The tests are for practice and to reinforce learning, and you may wish to test exam techniques and working to a set time limit. Using the mixed papers, we would recommend your child spends 35 minutes to answer the 64 questions in each Mixed paper. You can reduce the suggested time by five minutes to practise working at speed.

Using the Progress Chart

The Progress Chart can be used to track focus test and mixed paper results over time to monitor how well your child is doing and identify any repeated problems in tackling the different question types.

Focus test 1 — Similarities

Which of the shapes belongs to the group on the left? Circle the letter.

Example

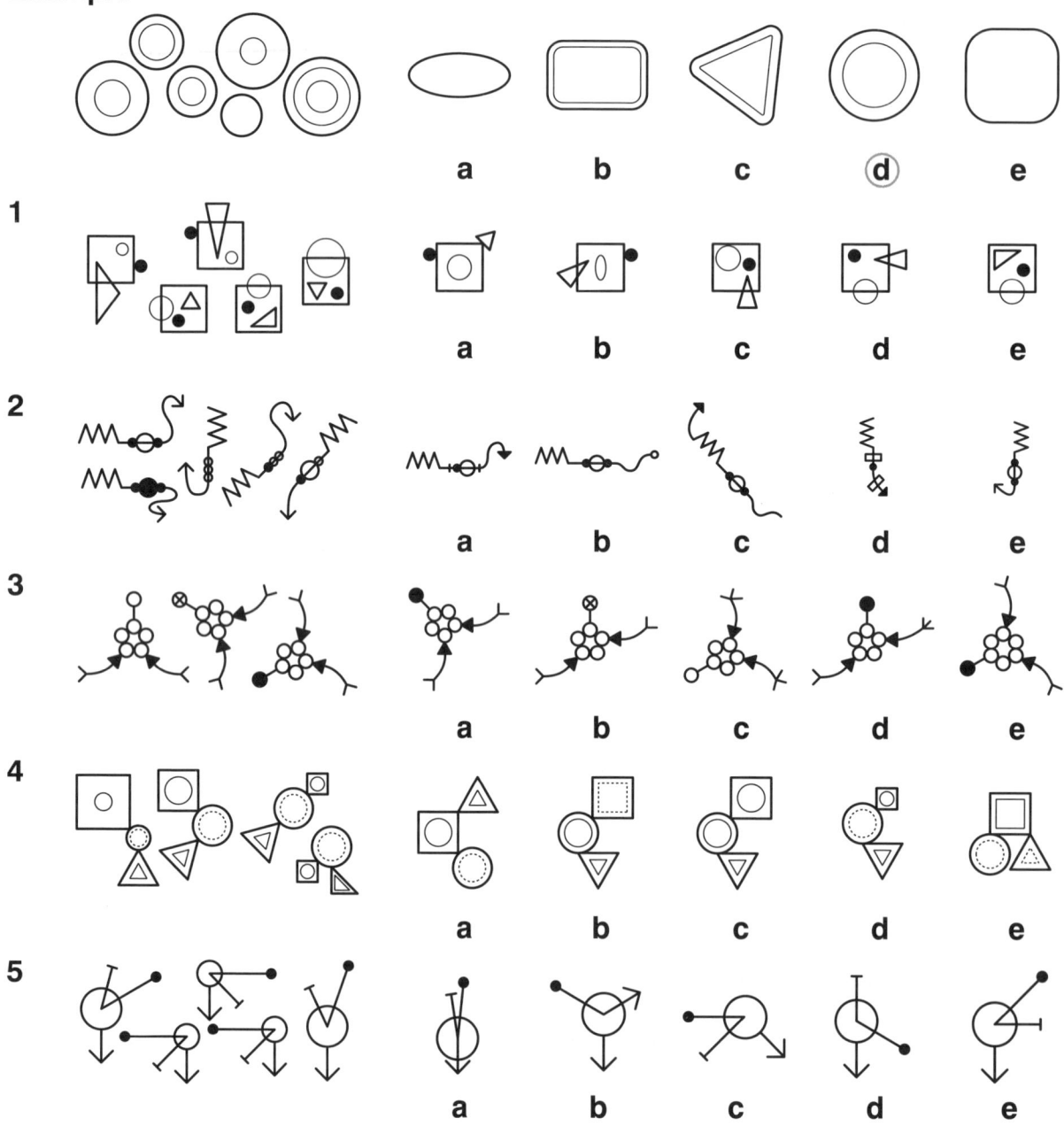

a b c (d) e

1
a b c d e

2
a b c d e

3
a b c d e

4
a b c d e

5
a b c d e

If more than one option looks possible, select the one that gives the best or closest match.

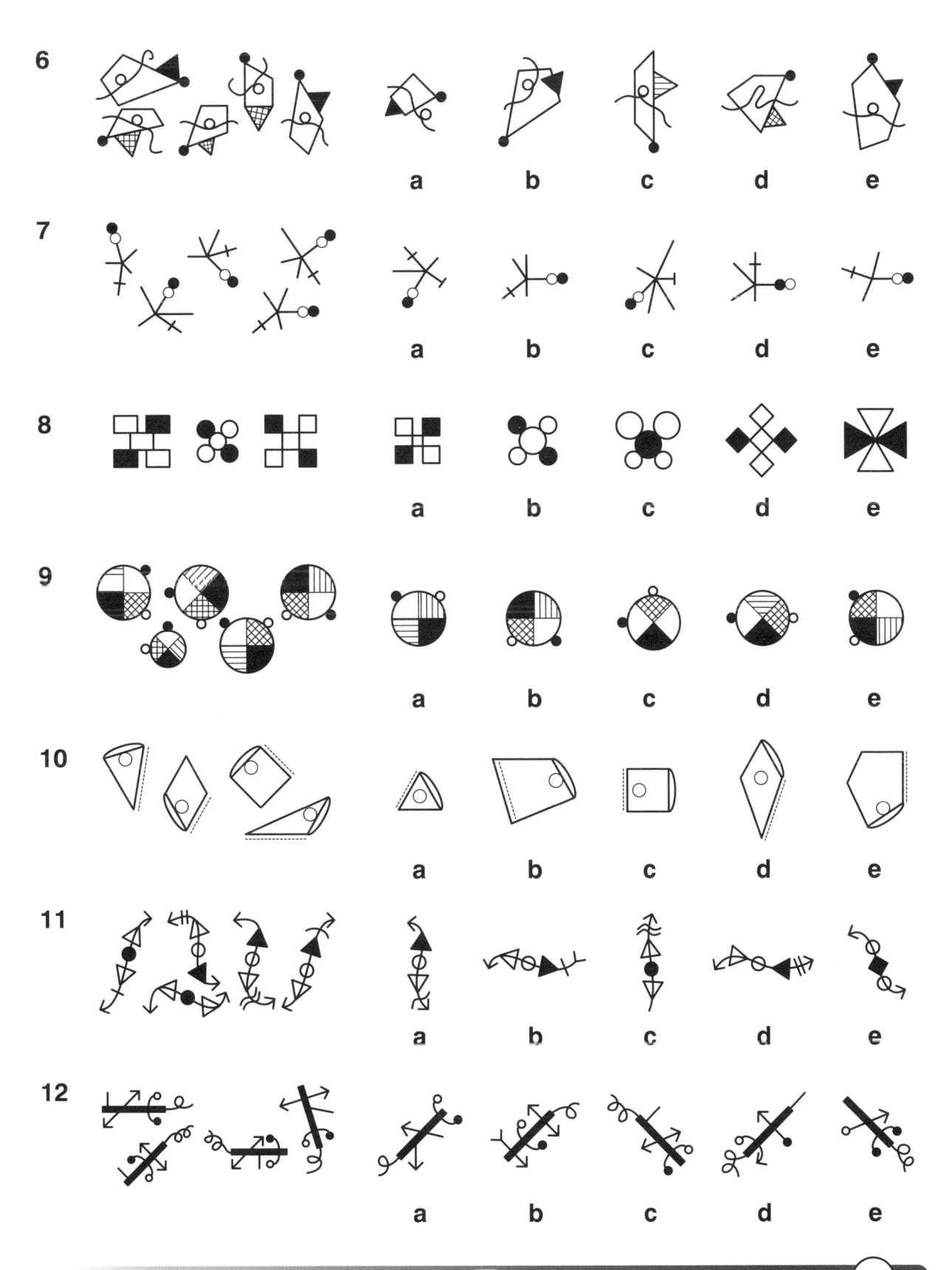

6

a b c d e

7

a b c d e

8

a b c d e

9

a b c d e

10

a b c d e

11

a b c d e

12

a b c d e

Now go to the Progress Chart ... 5 *... to record your score!* Total 12

Focus test 2 — Grids

Which shape or pattern completes the pattern on the left? Circle the letter.

Example

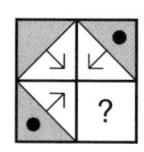

When looking at grids remember the patterns or sequences may go across the rows, down the columns or both ...

1.

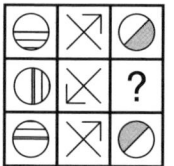

2.

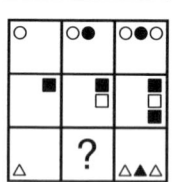

... or the whole grid may have a pattern.

3.

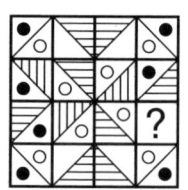

4.

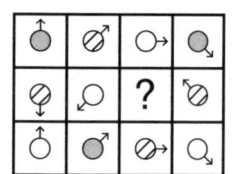

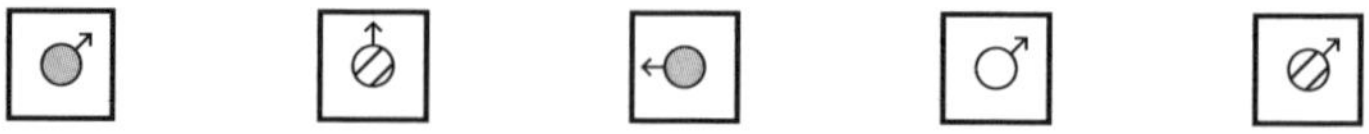

A sequence may continue from one row to the next.

5.

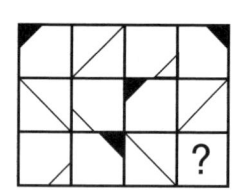

6   a   b   c   d   e

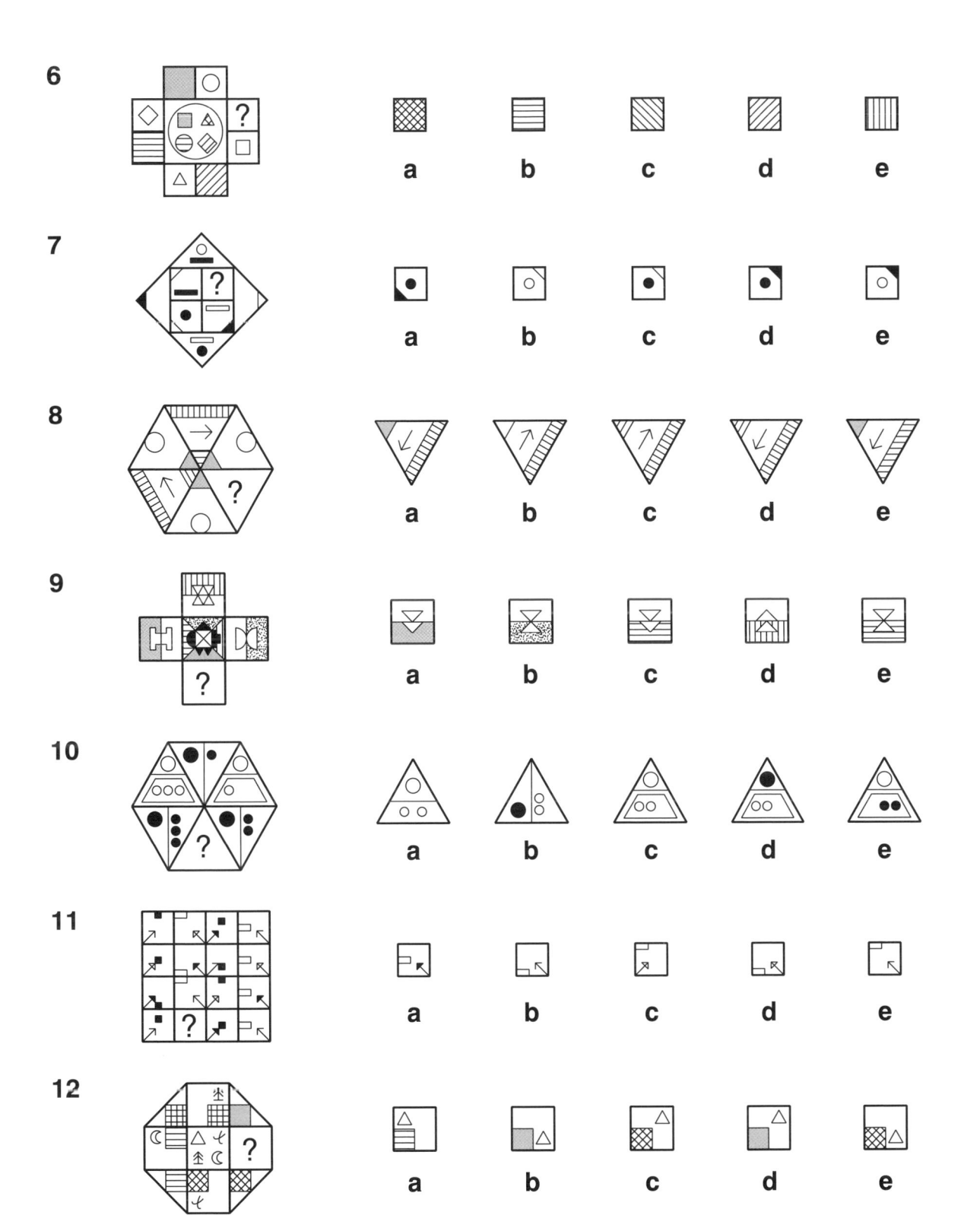

7   a   b   c   d   e

8   a   b   c   d   e

9   a   b   c   d   e

10   a   b   c   d   e

11   a   b   c   d   e

12   a   b   c   d   e

Now go to the Progress Chart ... **7** *... to record your score!*   Total 12

Focus test 3 — Analogies

Which shape or pattern completes the second pair in the same way as the first pair? Circle the letter.

Example

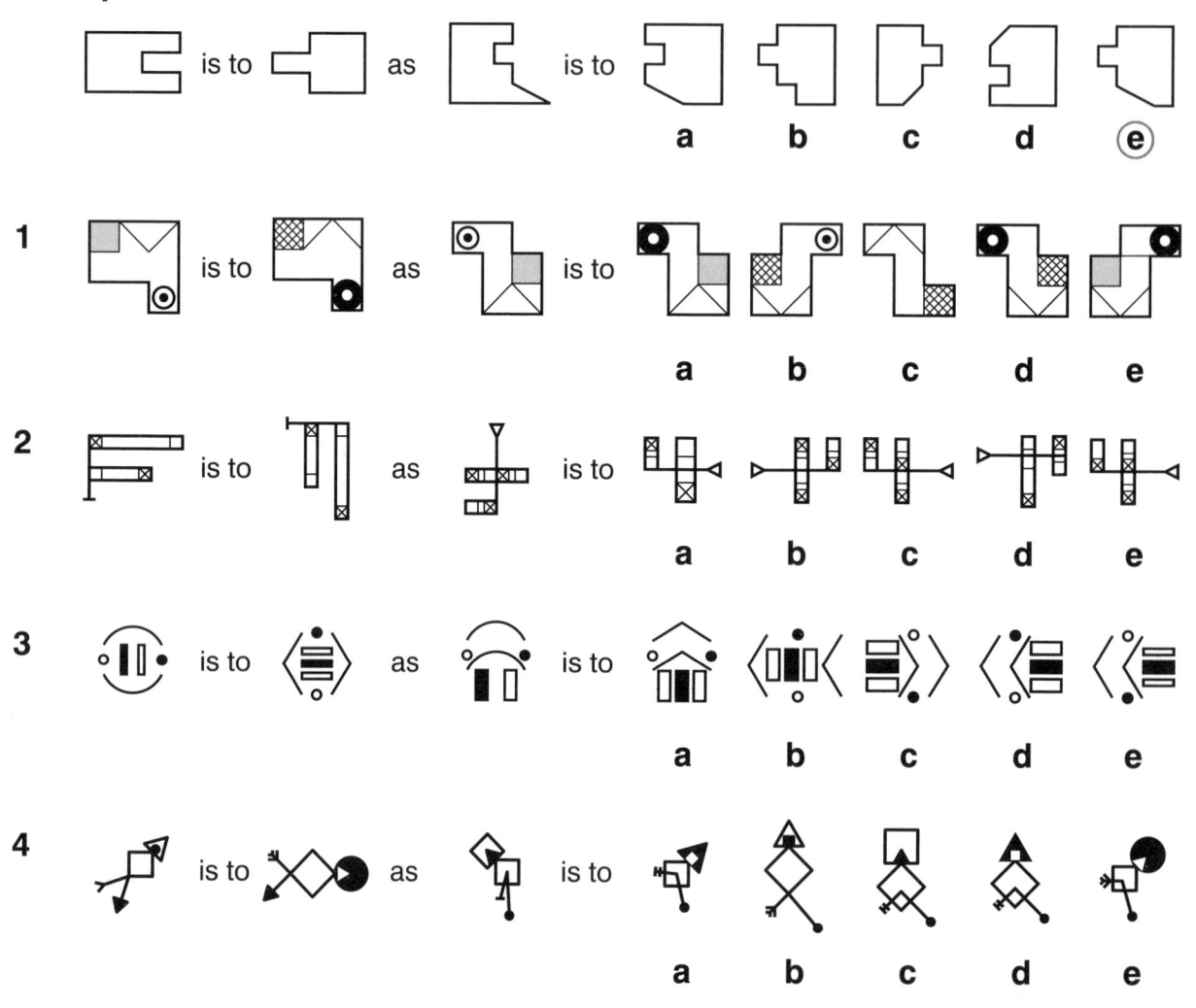

(answer: e)

1.

2.

3.

4.

> If you think that you can give a reason for more than one answer being correct, look carefully again at the first given pair and then choose the closest match.

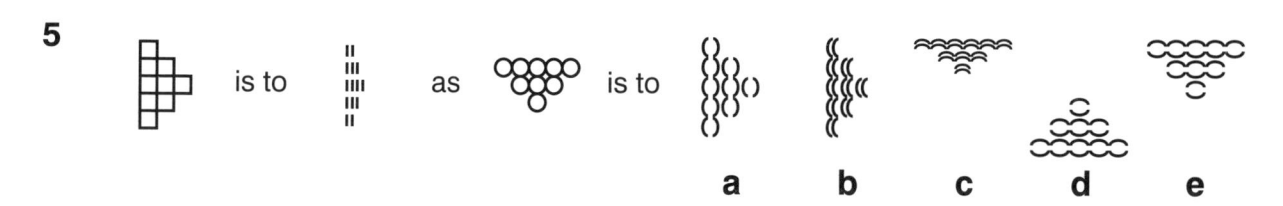

5.

6   a   b   c   d   e

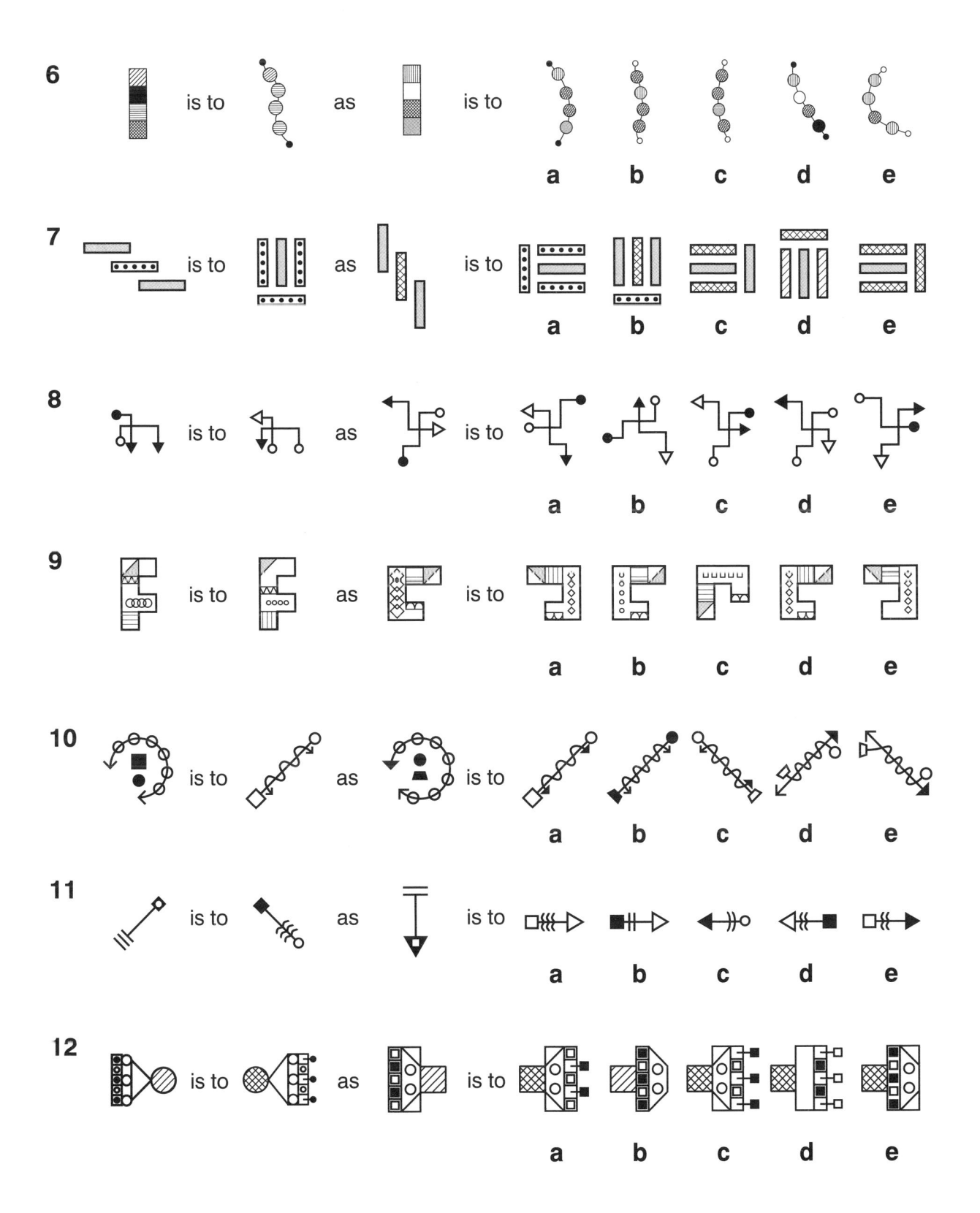

7   a   b   c   d   e

8   a   b   c   d   e

9   a   b   c   d   e

10   a   b   c   d   e

11   a   b   c   d   e

12   a   b   c   d   e

Now go to the Progress Chart ... 9 *... to record your score!*   Total   12

Focus test 4 — Reflections

Which shape or pattern is a reflection of the shape on the left? Circle the letter.

Example

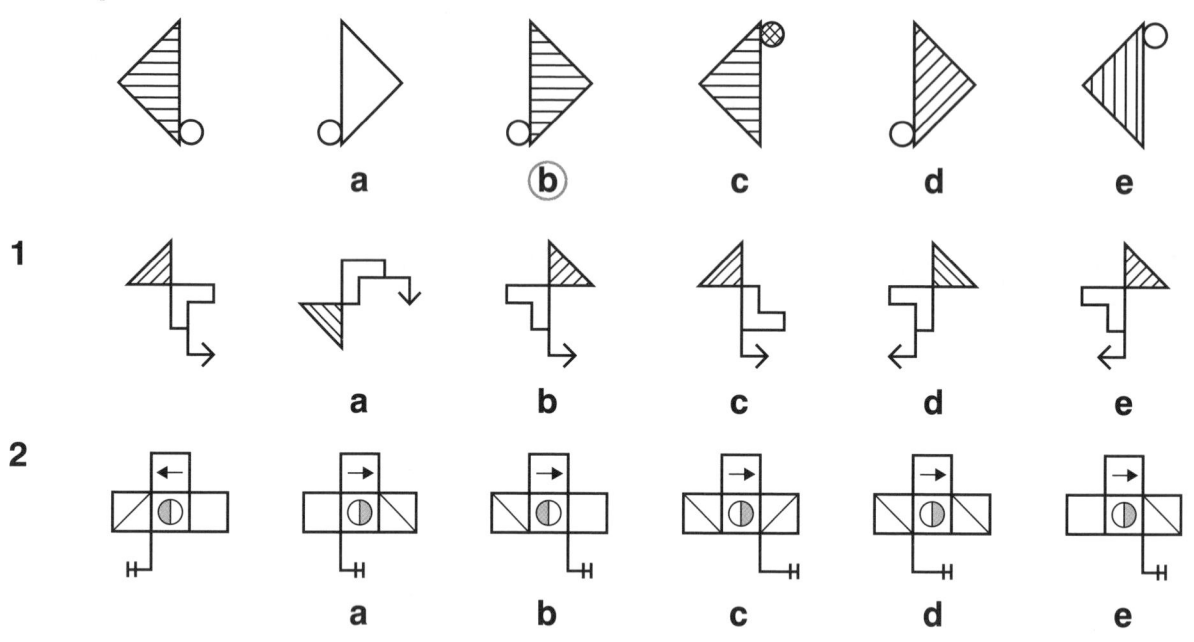

a　b　c　d　e

1

a　b　c　d　e

2

a　b　c　d　e

> The line of reflection for these patterns may be above, below or at either side of the shape or pattern.

3

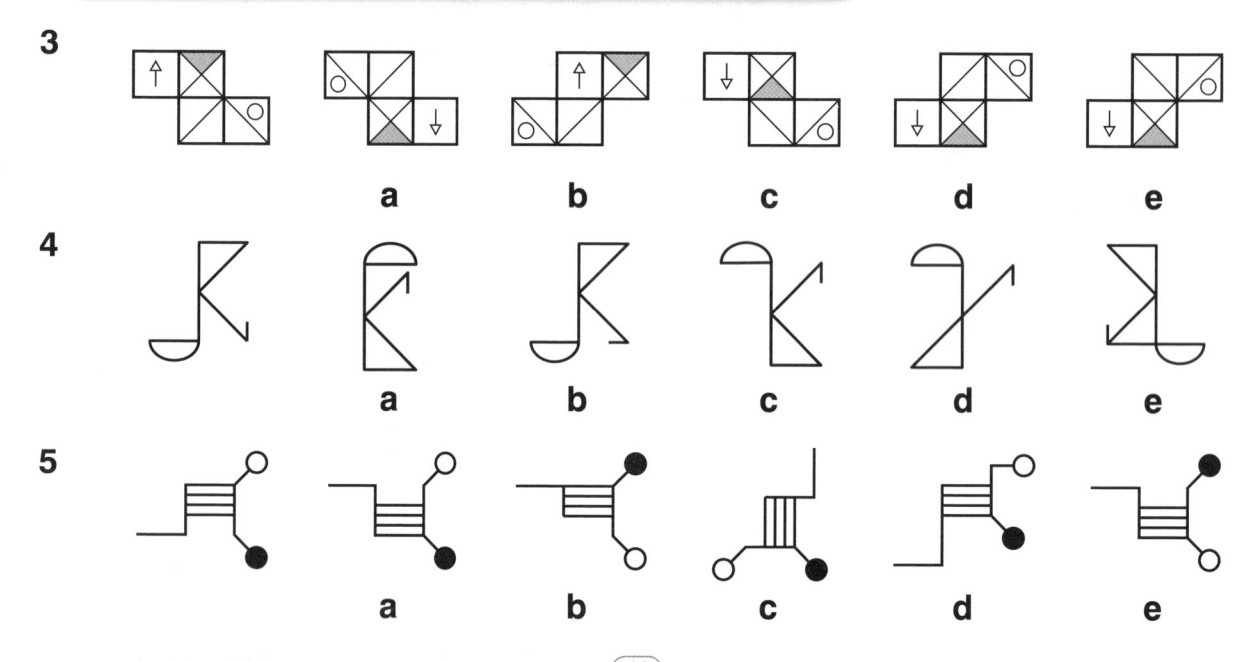

a　b　c　d　e

4

a　b　c　d　e

5

a　b　c　d　e

The line of reflection may also be on the diagonal.

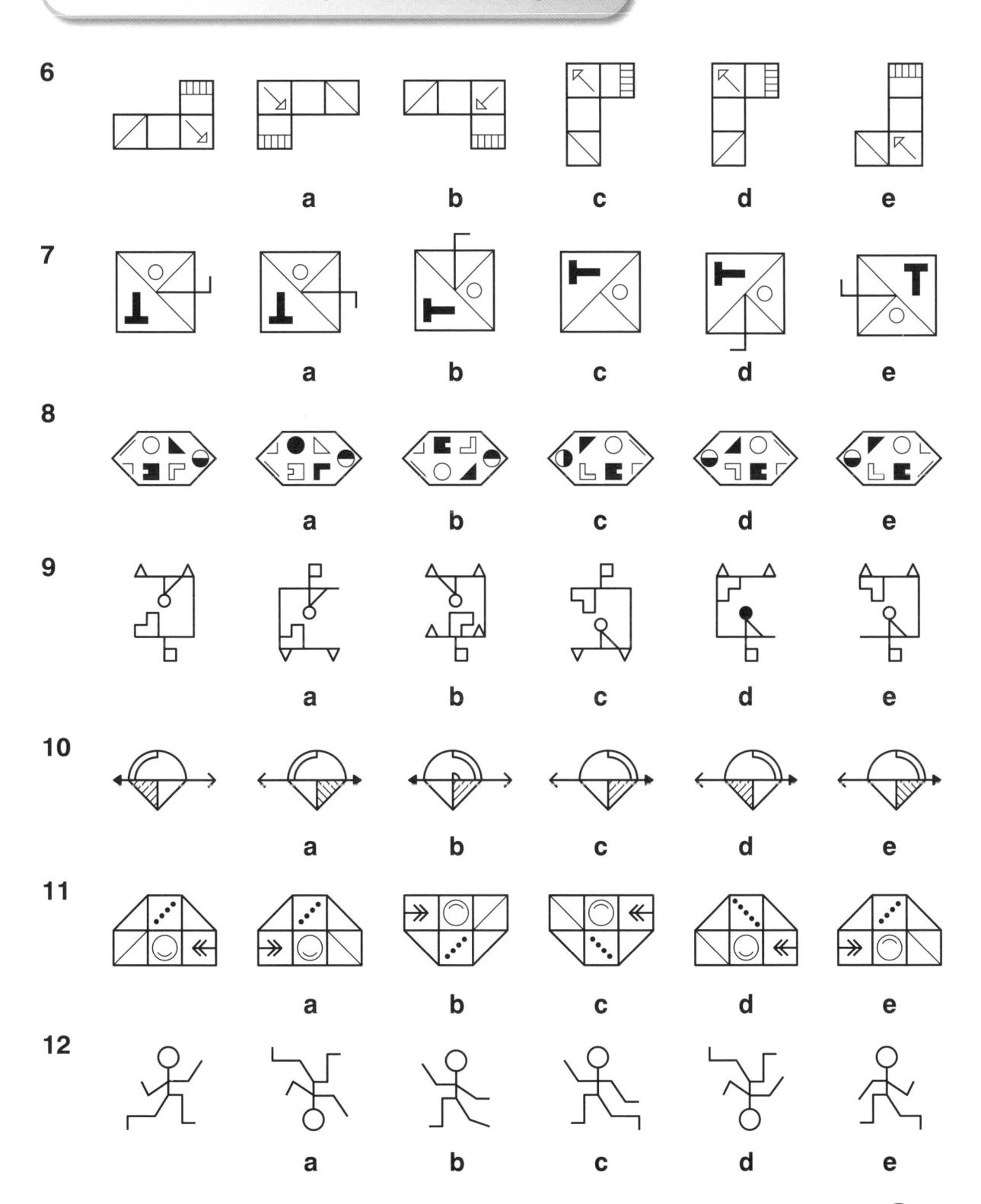

Focus test 5 — Sequences

Which shape or pattern continues or completes the given sequence? Circle the letter.

Example

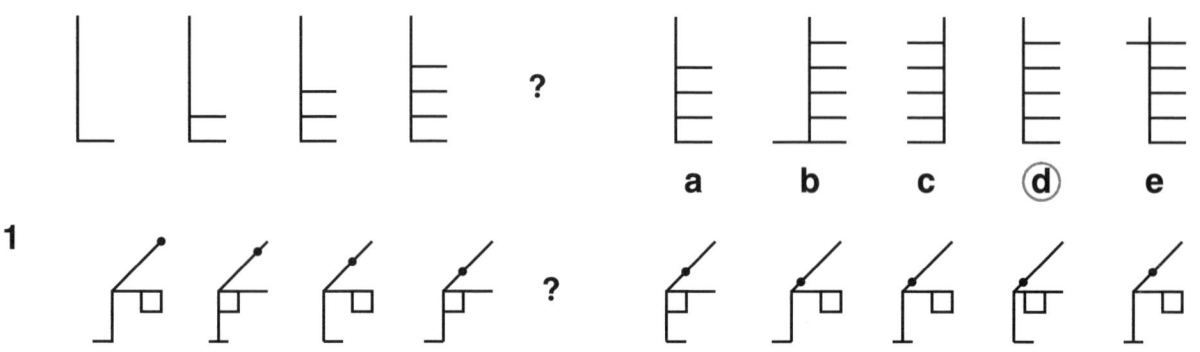

a b c ⓓ e

1.

a b c d e

A sequence may be made up of two different sequences alternating.

2.

a b c d e

3.

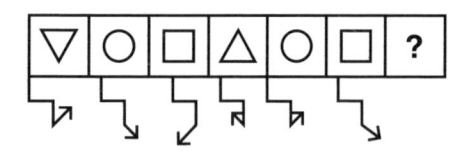

a b c d e

To fill a gap in a sequence work forward and then check by also looking back.

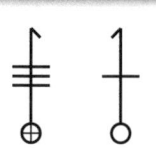

4.

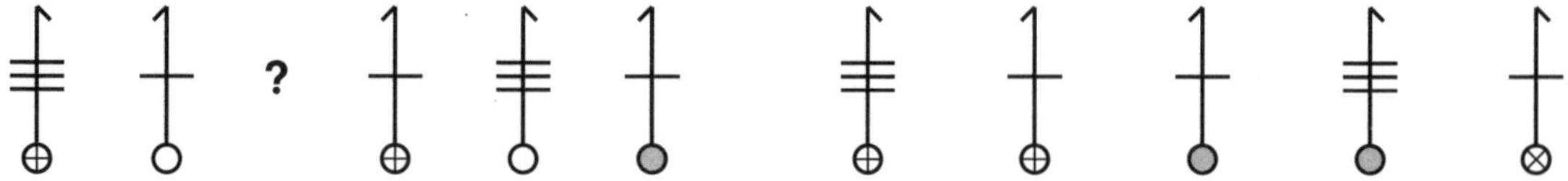

a b c d e

5.

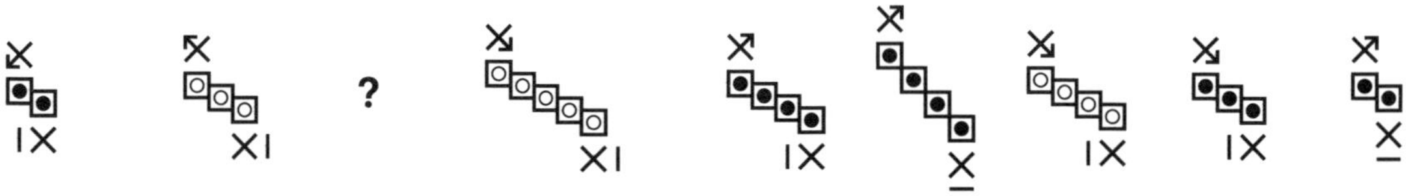

a b c d e

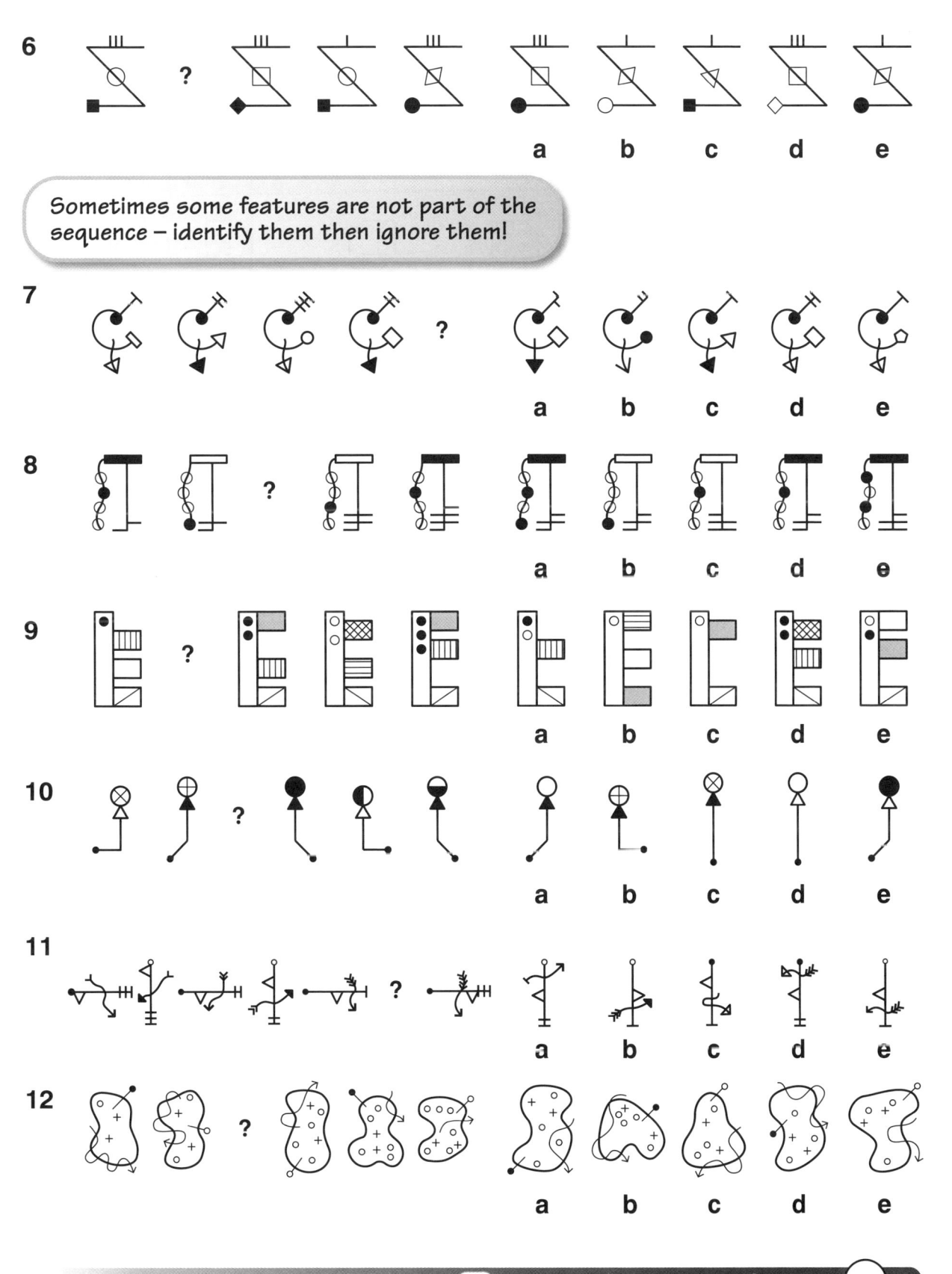

6

Sometimes some features are not part of the sequence – identify them then ignore them!

7

8

9

10

11

12

Now go to the Progress Chart ... 13 ... to record your score! Total 12

Focus test 6 — Cubes

Which cube could not be made from the given net? Circle the letter.

Example

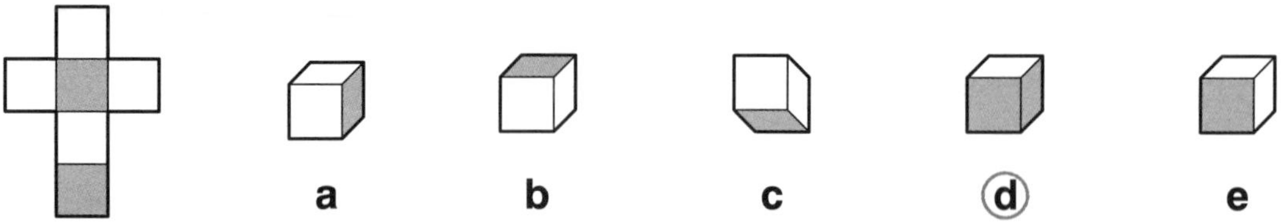

a   b   c   (d)   e

> For each type of net, identify the faces that could not end up adjacent (next to each other) in the cube. Always look carefully at the direction of any arrows or shading lines.

1 a b c d e

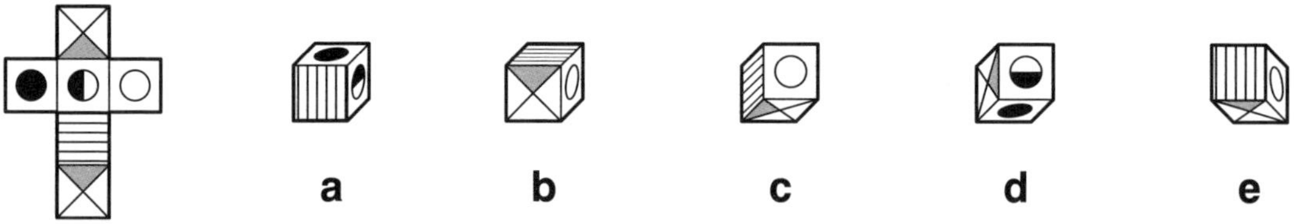

2 a b c d e

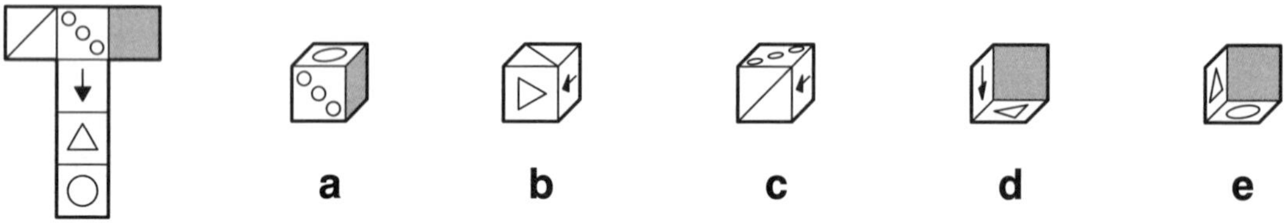

3 a b c d e

4 a b c d e

5 a b c d e

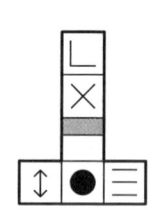

6 7 8 9 10 11 12

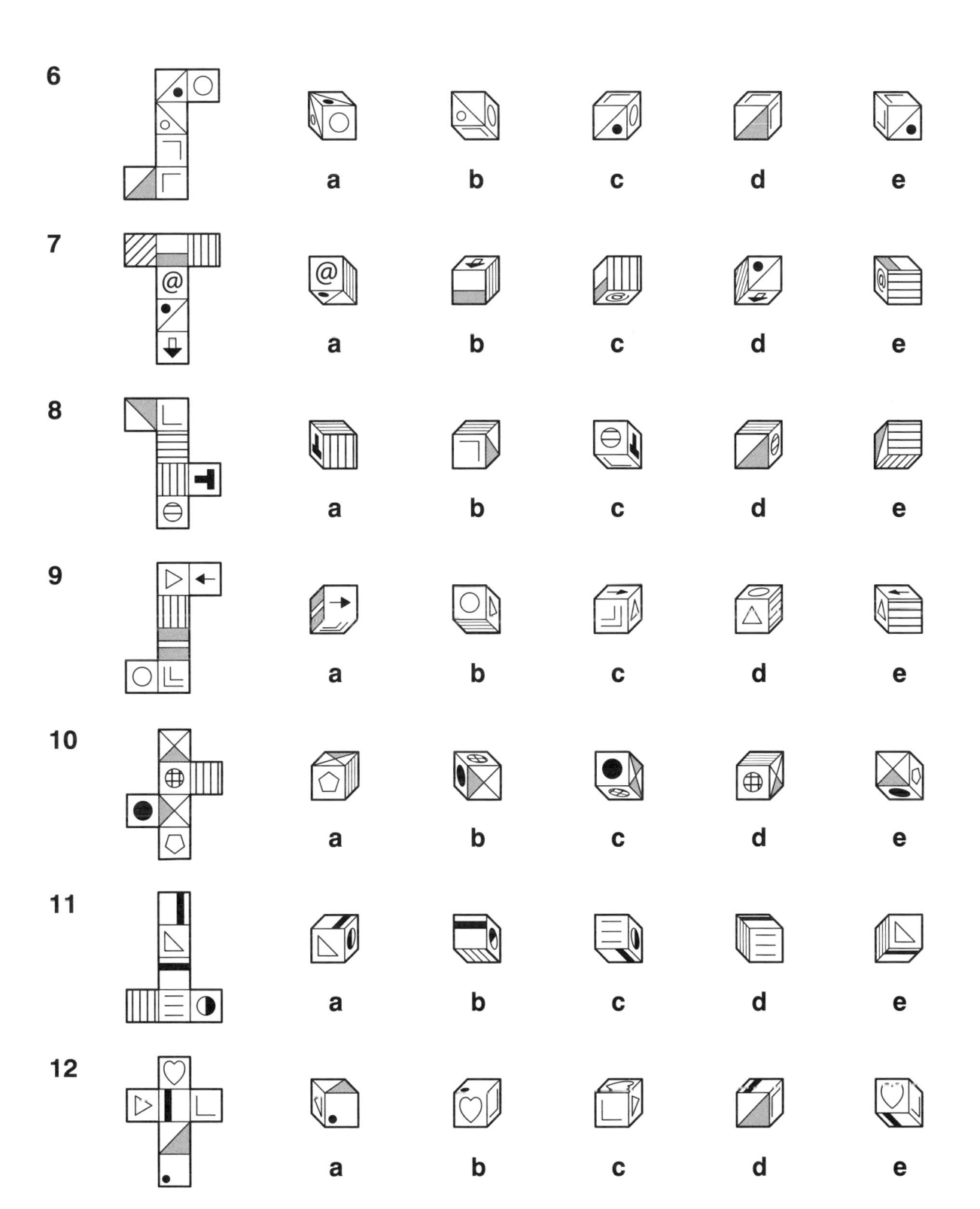

a b c d e

Focus test 7 — Codes

Using the given patterns and codes, work out the code that matches the last pattern. Circle the letter.

Example

						AZ	CX	CZ	BY	CY
AX	AY	BZ	CY	BX	?	a	b	ⓒ	d	e

> At this level you may have to work out codes by deduction, they are not always in the examples given.

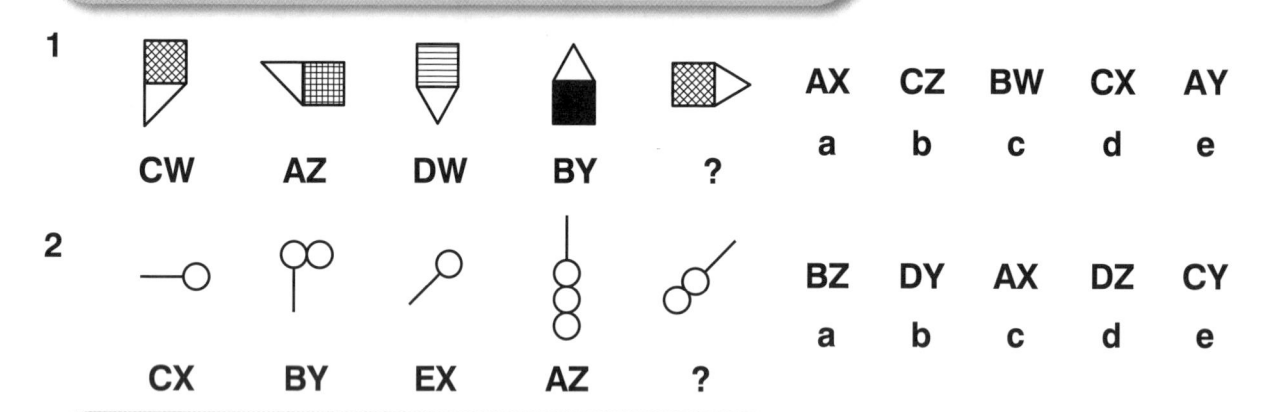

1

						AX	CZ	BW	CX	AY
CW	AZ	DW	BY	?		a	b	c	d	e

2

						BZ	DY	AX	DZ	CY
CX	BY	EX	AZ	?		a	b	c	d	e

> Extra features may be added that are not linked to the code – don't be distracted by them!

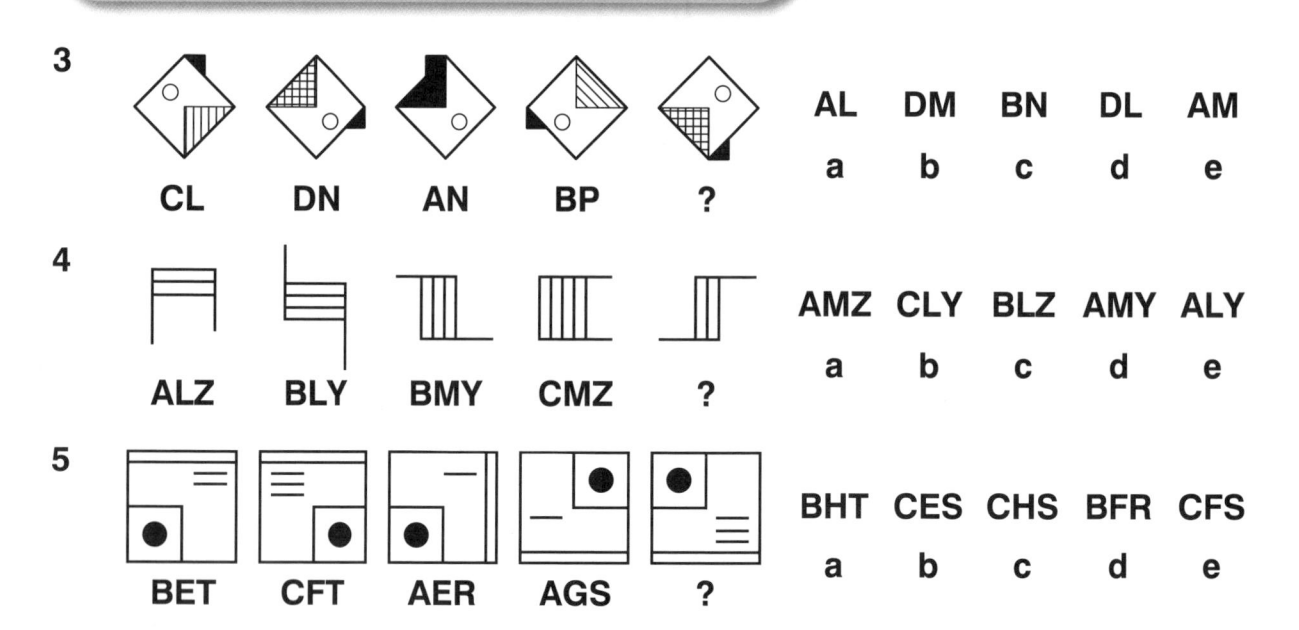

3

						AL	DM	BN	DL	AM
CL	DN	AN	BP	?		a	b	c	d	e

4

						AMZ	CLY	BLZ	AMY	ALY
ALZ	BLY	BMY	CMZ	?		a	b	c	d	e

5

						BHT	CES	CHS	BFR	CFS
BET	CFT	AER	AGS	?		a	b	c	d	e

Sometimes part of the code appears to be able to link with one or two different features – the answer options may help you to identify the correct one.

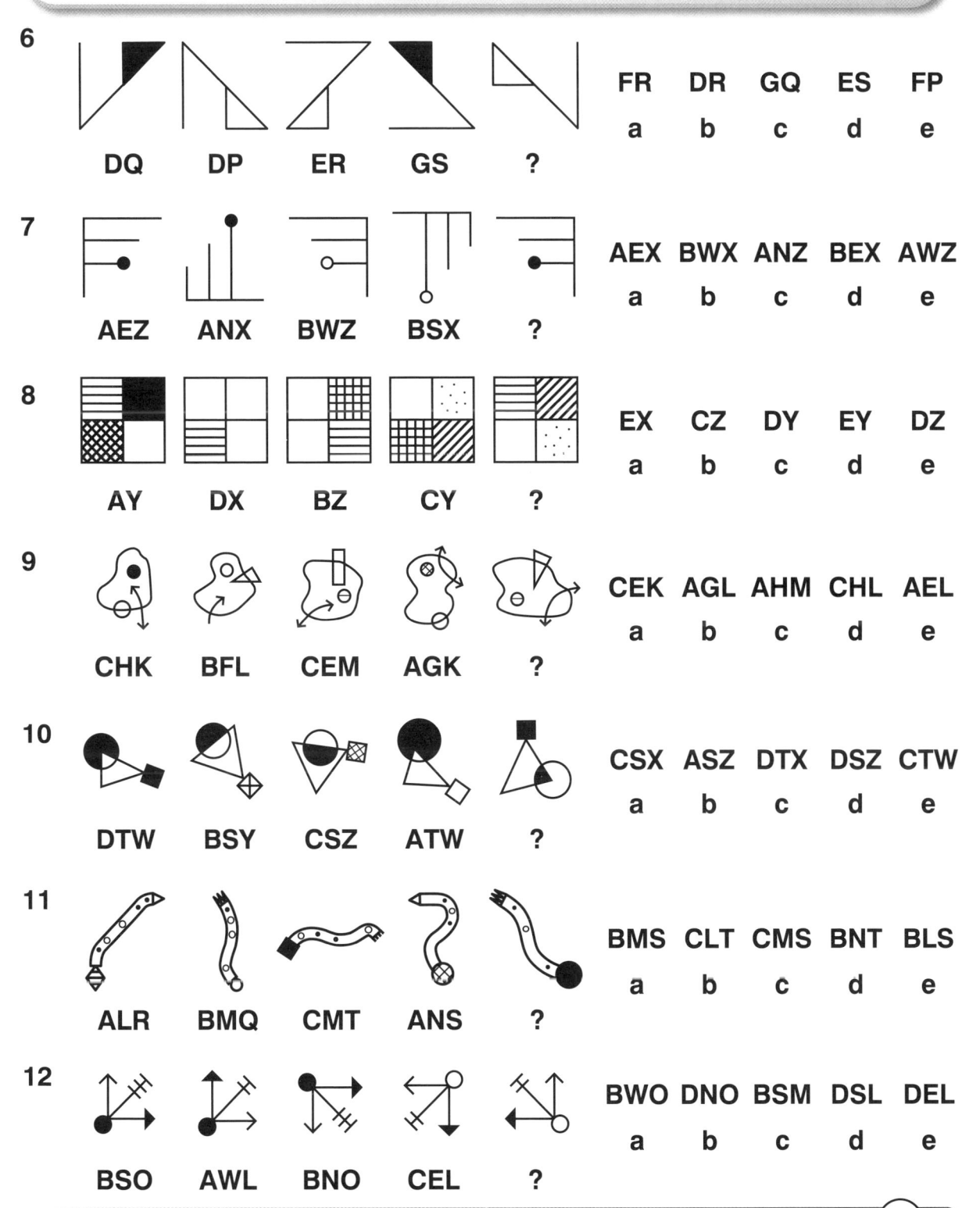

6

DQ DP ER GS ?

FR	DR	GQ	ES	FP
a	b	c	d	e

7

AEZ ANX BWZ BSX ?

AEX	BWX	ANZ	BEX	AWZ
a	b	c	d	e

8

AY DX BZ CY ?

EX	CZ	DY	EY	DZ
a	b	c	d	e

9

CHK BFL CEM AGK ?

CEK	AGL	AHM	CHL	AEL
a	b	c	d	e

10

DTW BSY CSZ ATW ?

CSX	ASZ	DTX	DSZ	CTW
a	b	c	d	e

11

ALR BMQ CMT ANS ?

BMS	CLT	CMS	BNT	BLS
a	b	c	d	e

12

BSO AWL BNO CEL ?

BWO	DNO	BSM	DSL	DEL
a	b	c	d	e

Focus test 8 — Combining Shapes

Which pattern on the right is formed by combining the two shapes on the left? Circle the letter.

Example

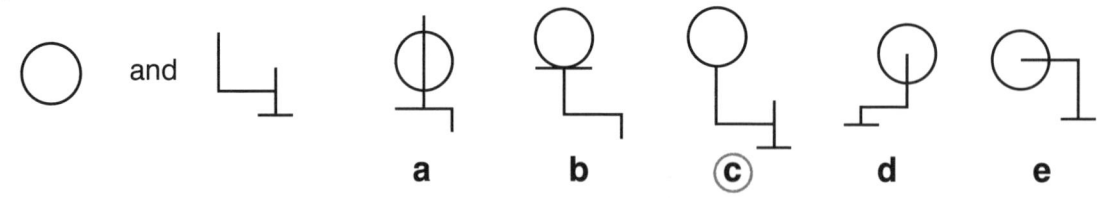

In these questions it is important to remember that patterns may be rotated, but not turned over – like jigsaw puzzle pieces.

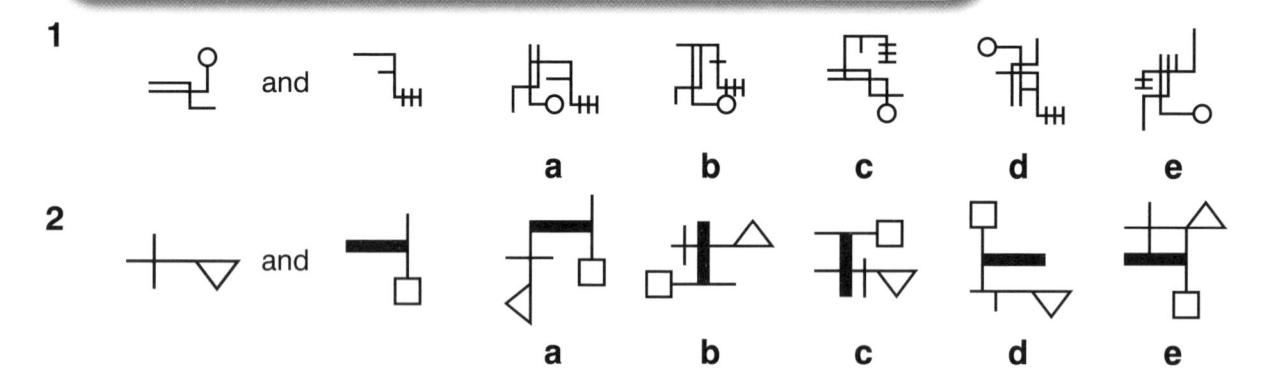

Separate 2-D shapes may share an edge in the combined shape, but line features will not overlap.

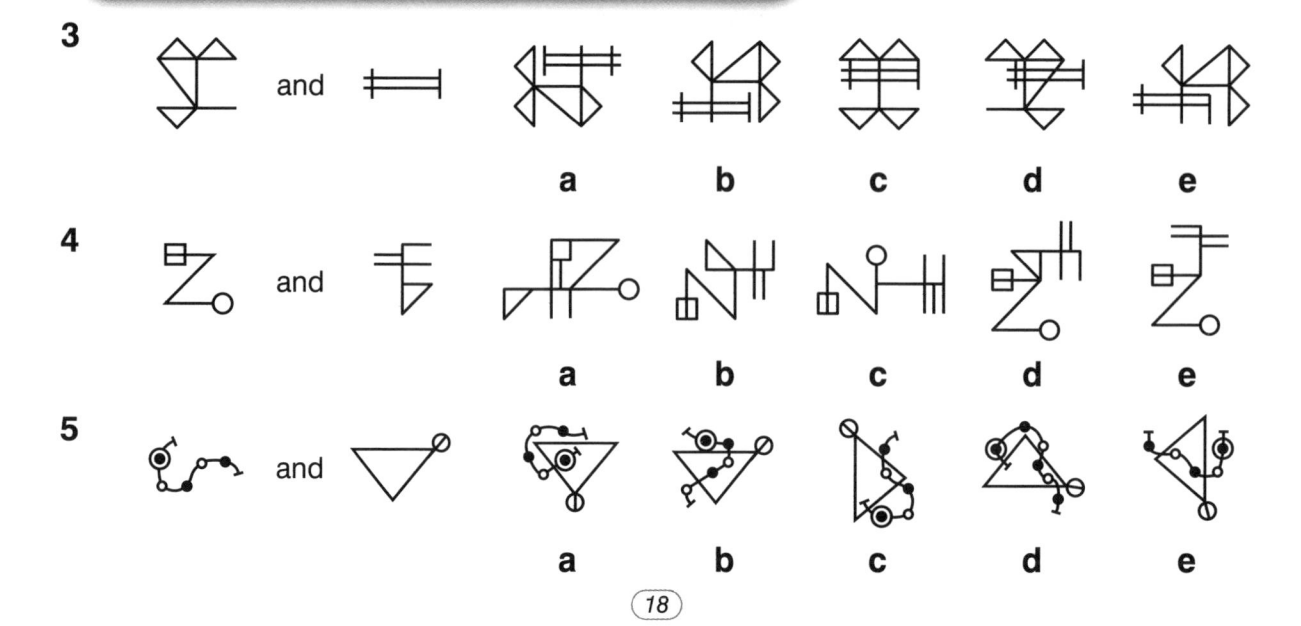

Always look very carefully at the angle and direction of any short branching lines.

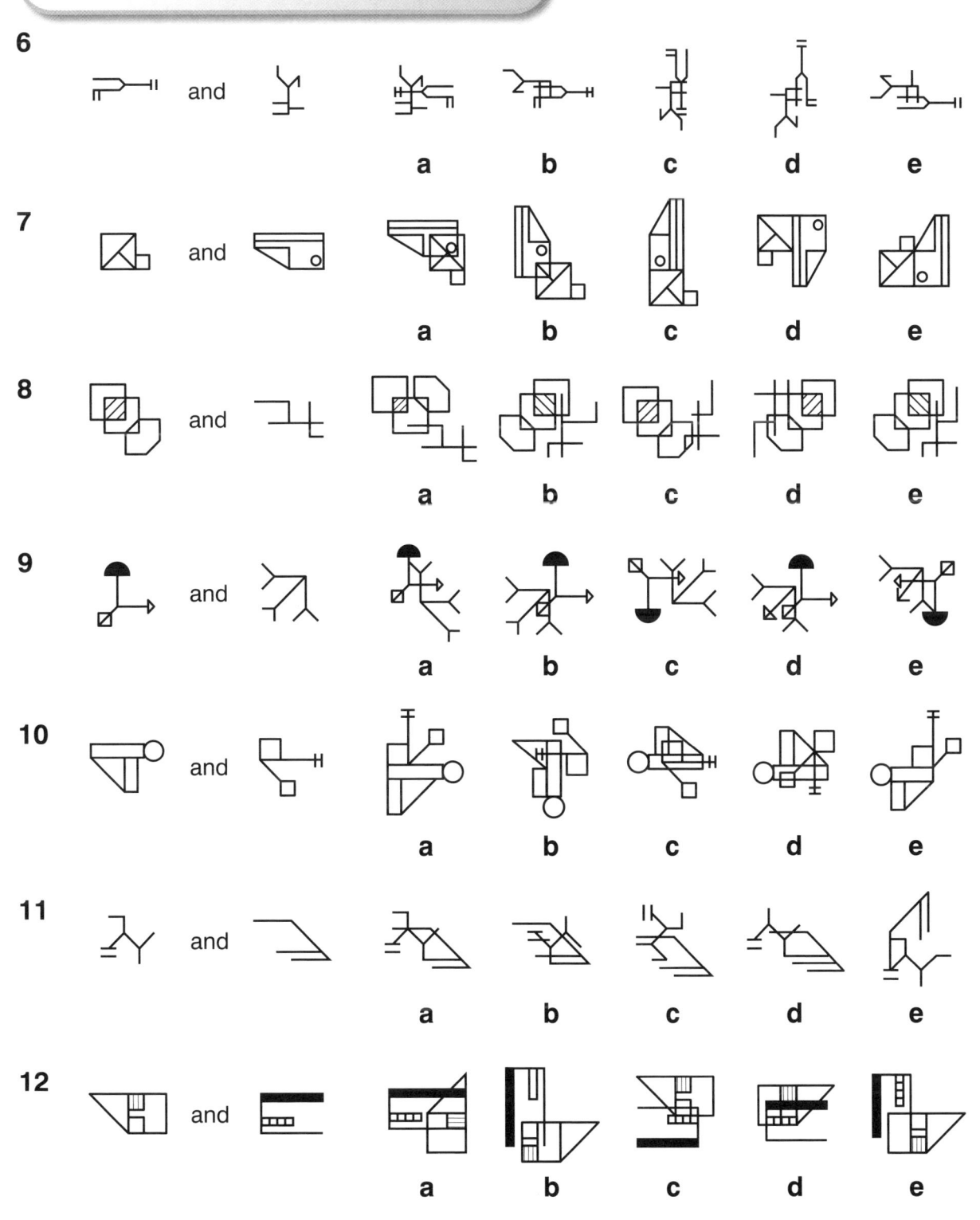

6

7

8

9

10

11

12

Now go to the Progress Chart ... 19 ... to record your score! Total 12

Mixed paper 1

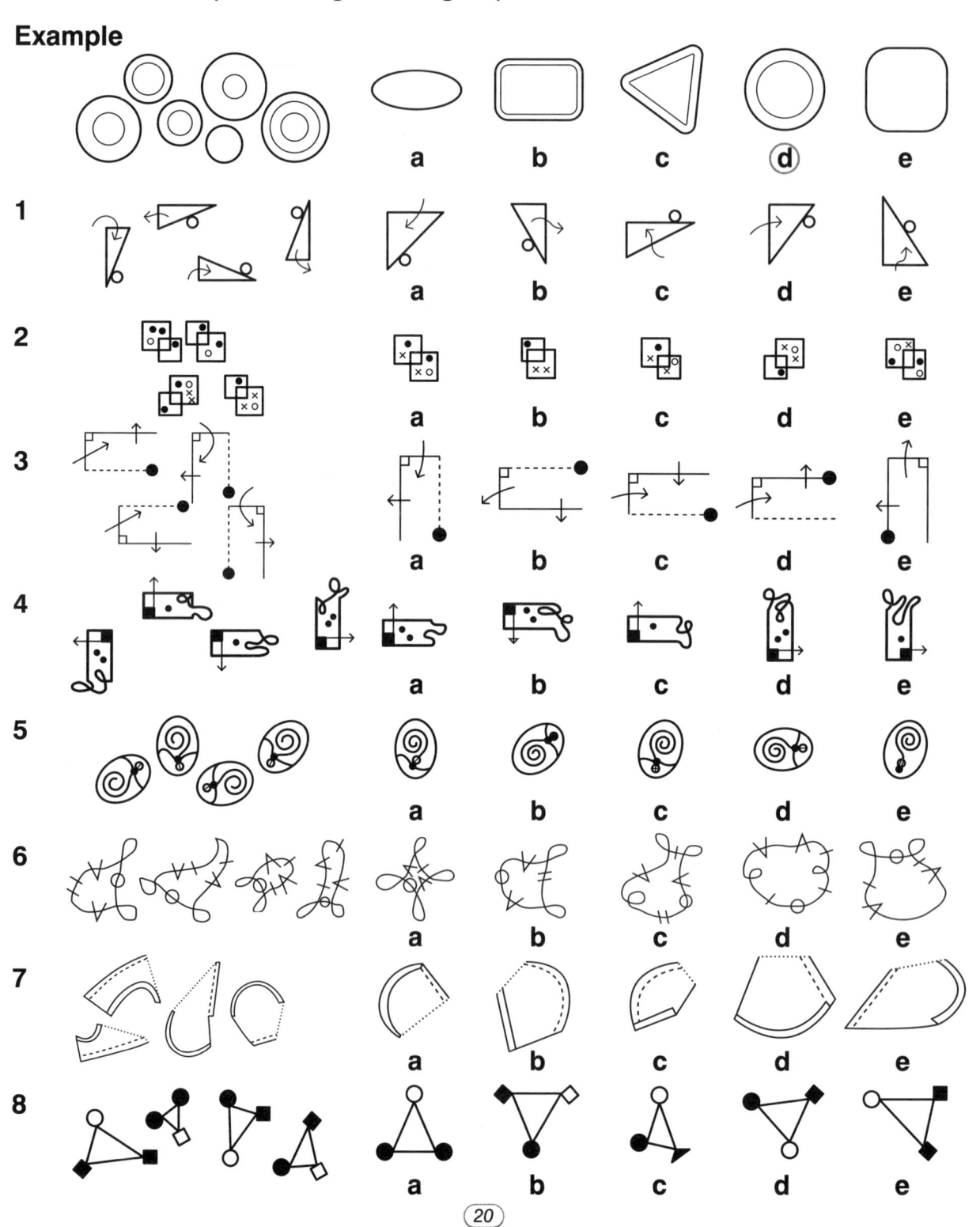

Which of the shapes belongs to the group on the left? Circle the letter.

Example

Which shape or pattern completes the pattern on the left? Circle the letter.

Example

a　b　c　d　e

9

a　b　c　d　e

10

a　b　c　d　e

11

a　b　c　d　e

12

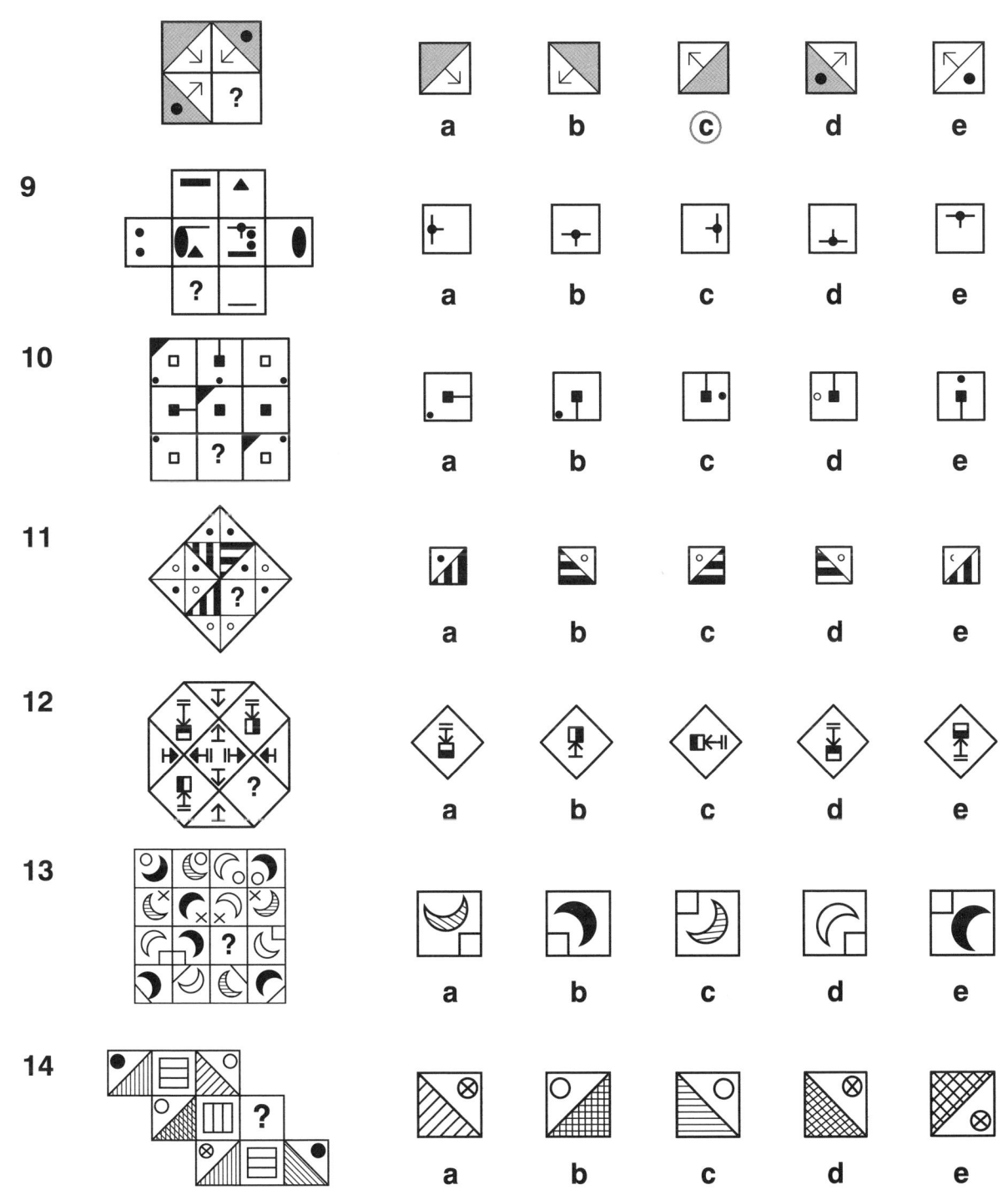

a　b　c　d　e

13

a　b　c　d　e

14

a　b　c　d　e

15.

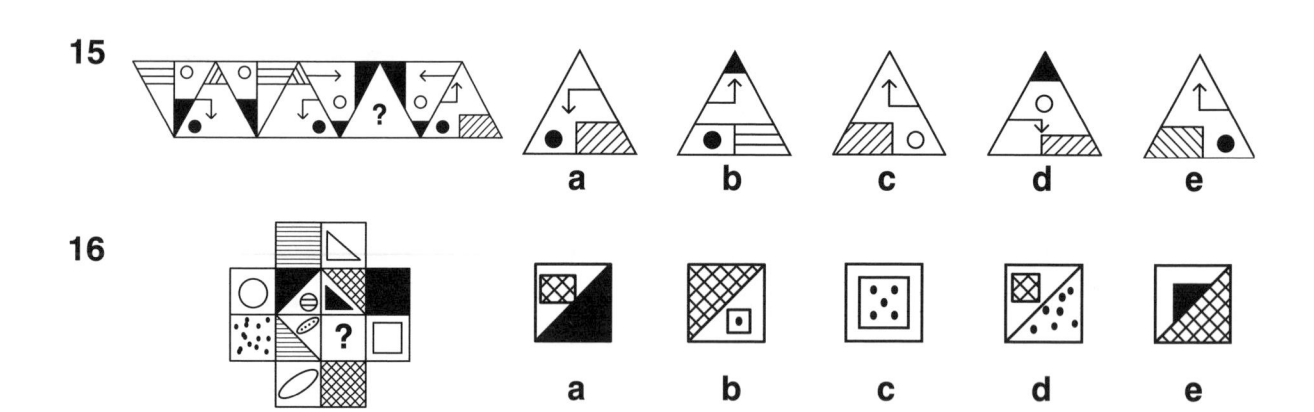

16.

Which shape or pattern completes the second pair in the same way as the first pair? Circle the letter.

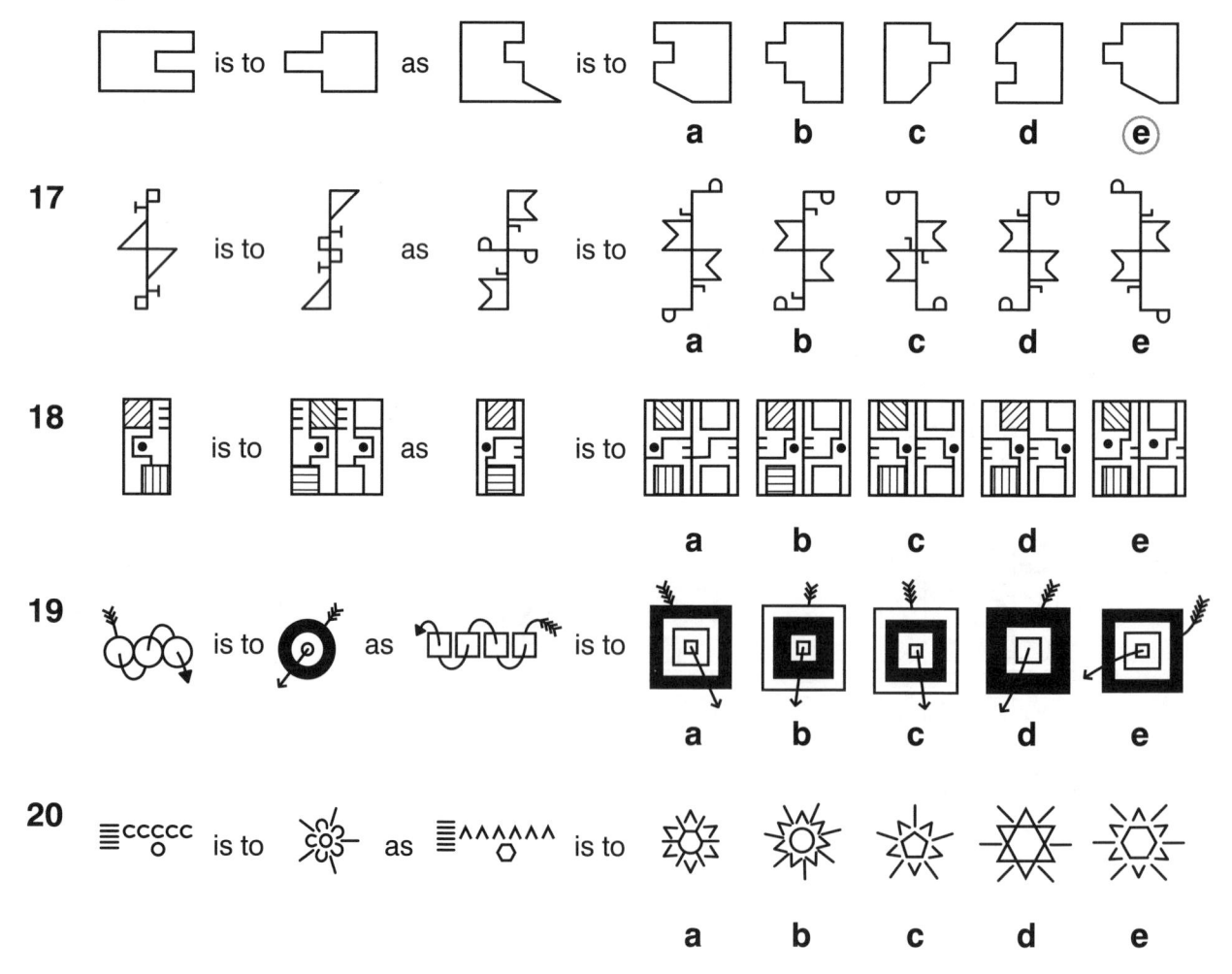

Example

is to … as … is to … a b c d (e)

17. is to … as … is to … a b c d e

18. is to … as … is to … a b c d e

19. is to … as … is to … a b c d e

20. is to … as … is to … a b c d e

21 ... a b c d e

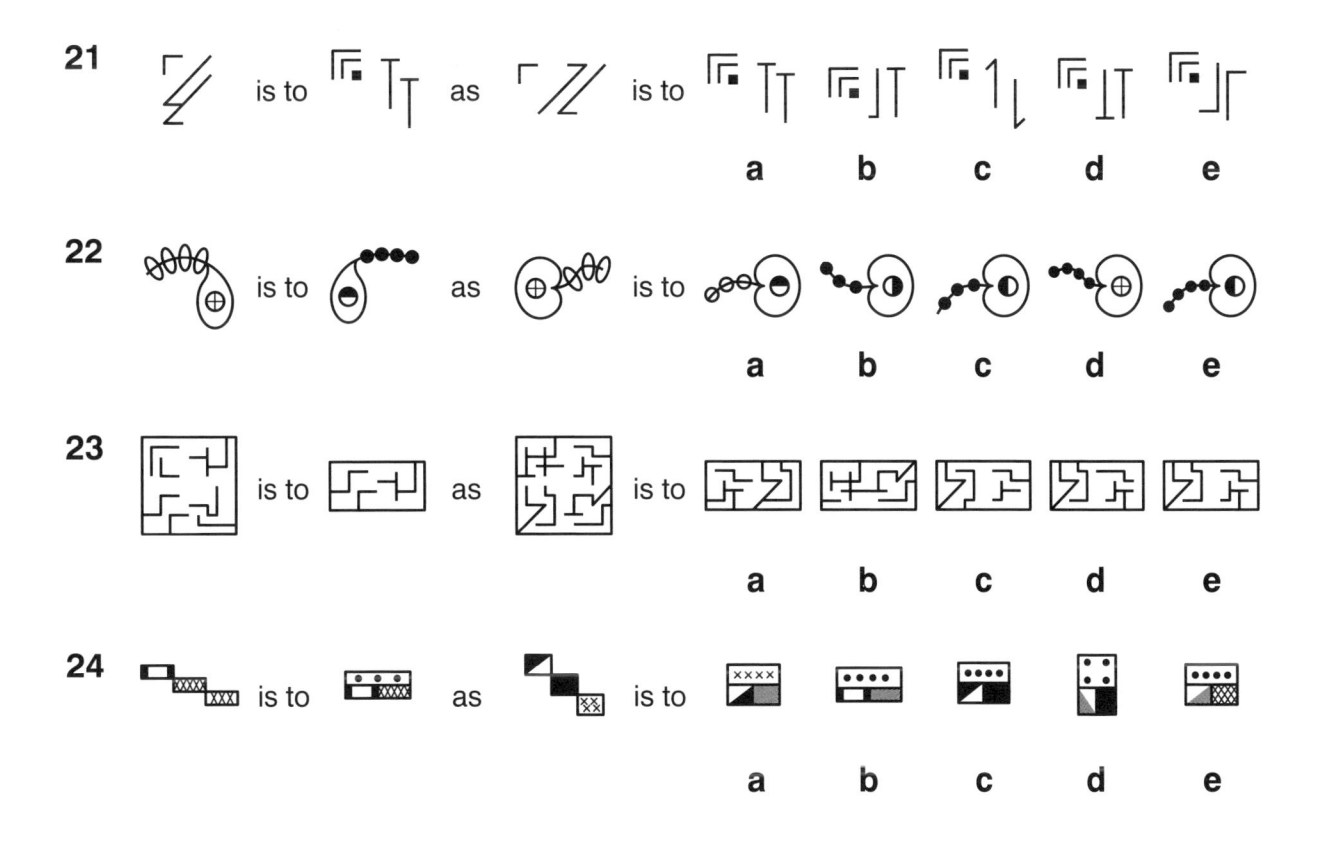

22 ... a b c d e

23 ... a b c d e

24 ... a b c d e

Which shape or pattern is a reflection of the shape on the left? Circle the letter.

Example

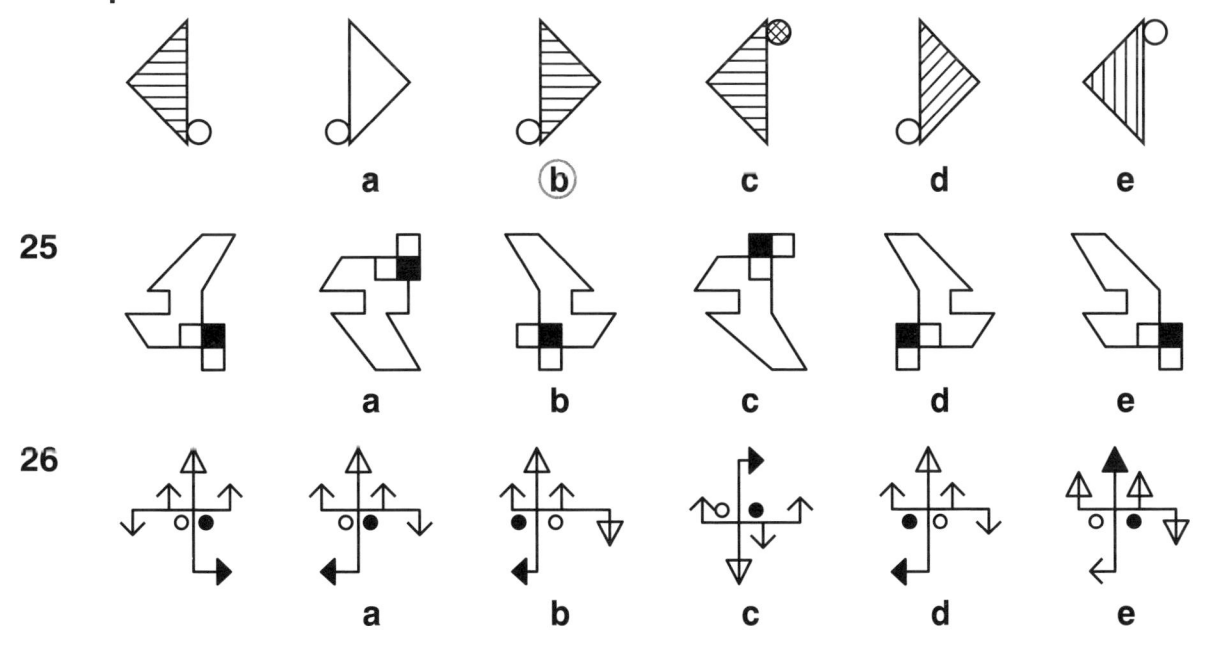

a (b) c d e

25 a b c d e

26 a b c d e

27

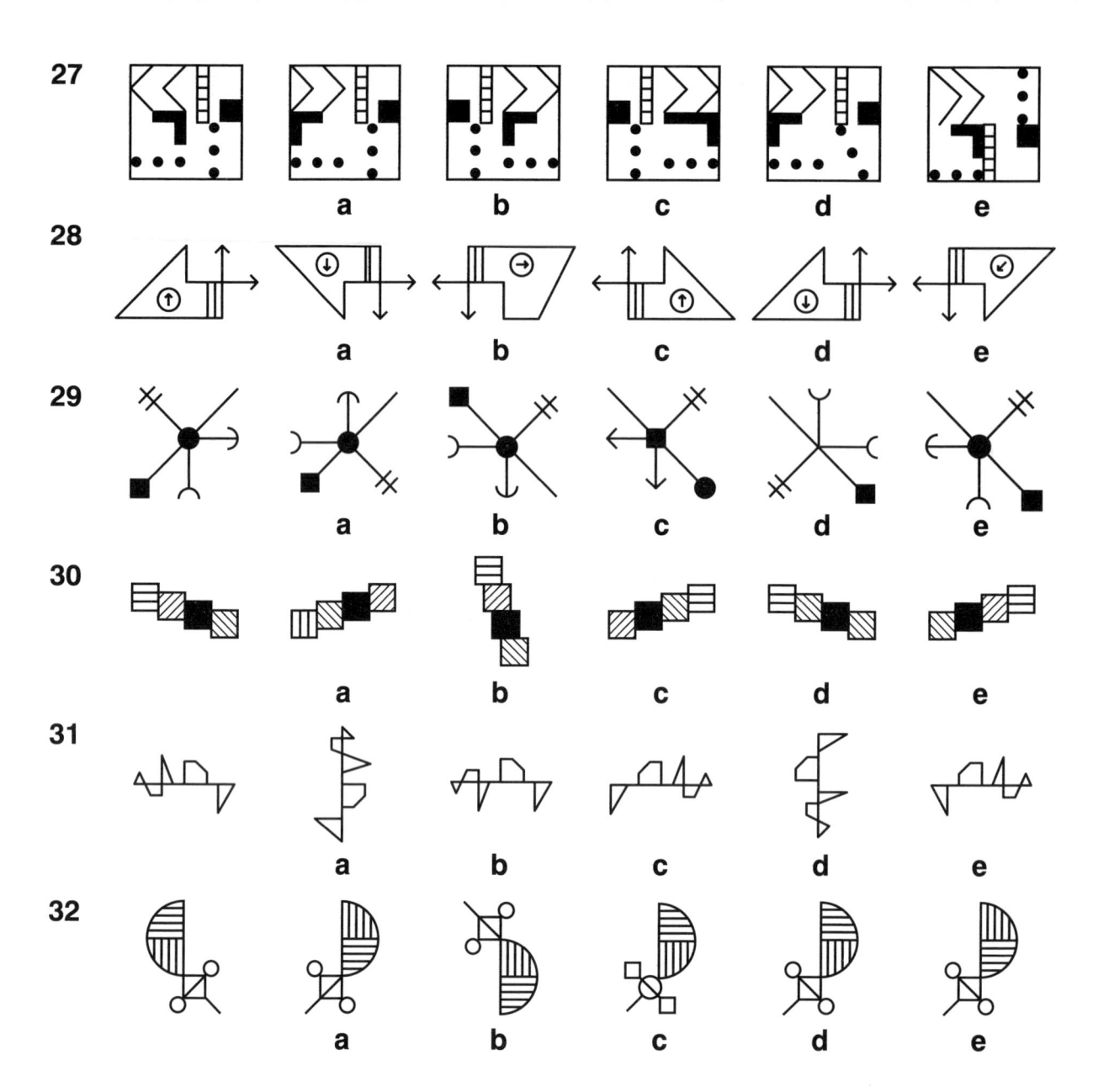

28

29

30

31

32

Which shape or pattern continues or completes the given sequence?
Circle the letter.

Example

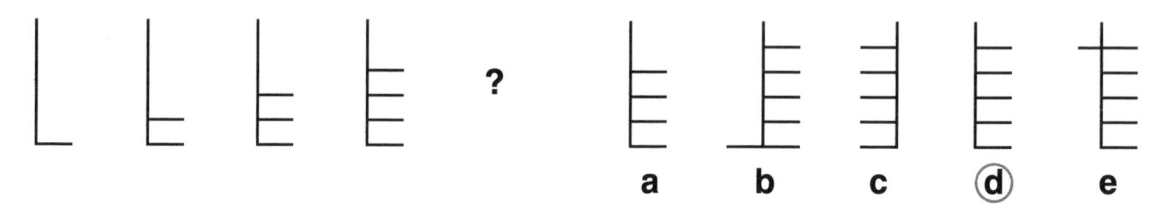

?   a   b   c   (d)   e

33
34
35
36
37
38
39
40

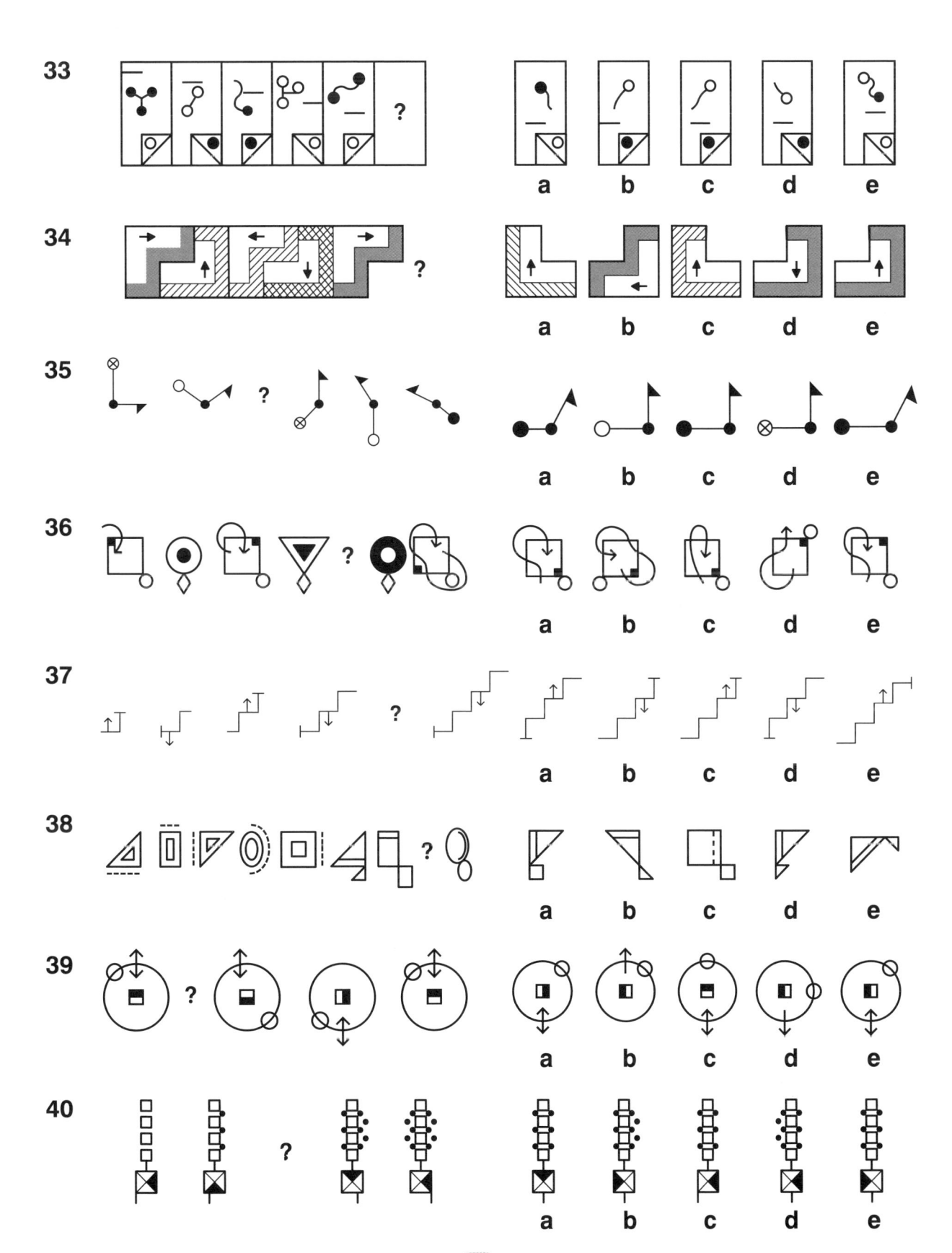

Which cube could not be made from the given net? Circle the letter.

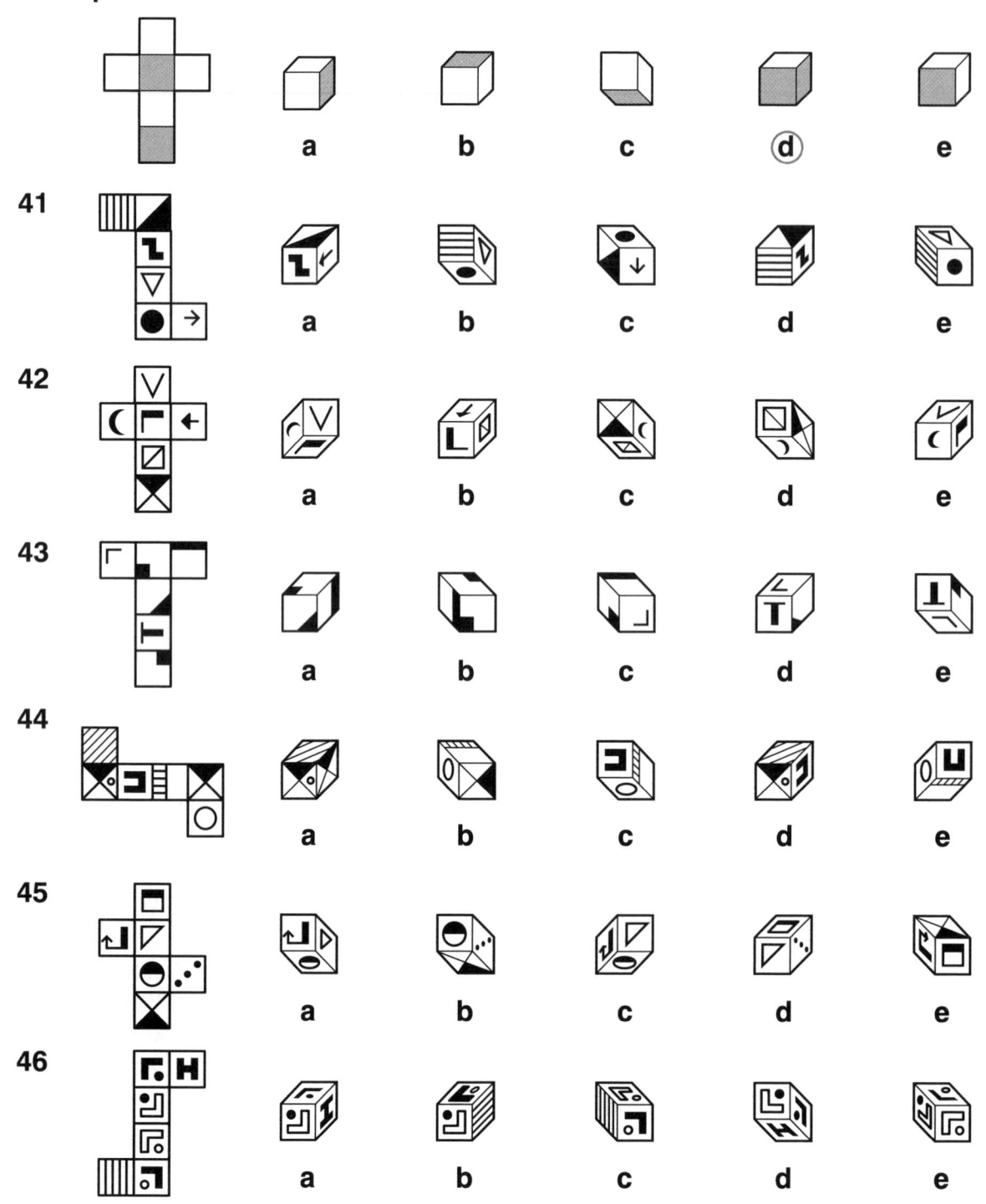

Example

a b c (d) e

41

a b c d e

42

a b c d e

43

a b c d e

44

a b c d e

45

a b c d e

46

a b c d e

47

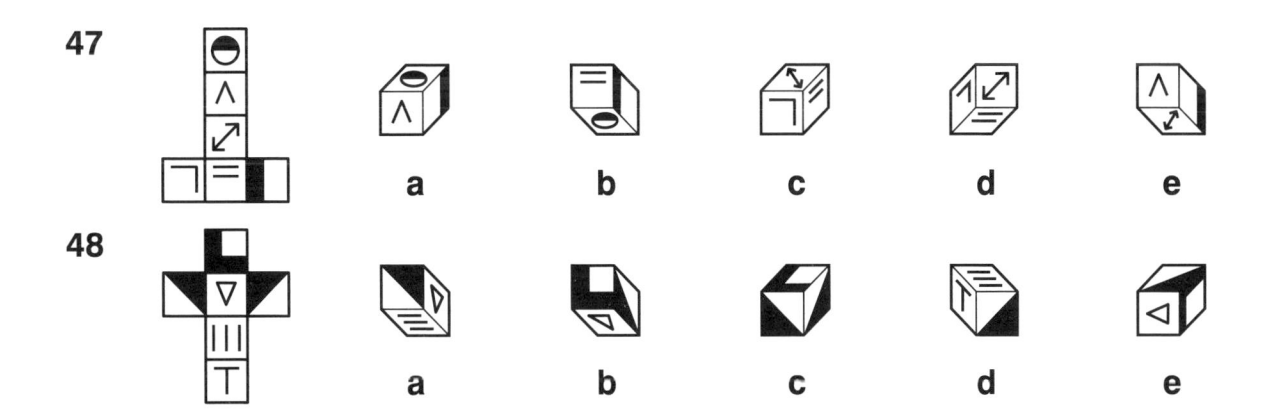

48

Using the given patterns and codes, work out the code that matches the last pattern. Circle the letter.

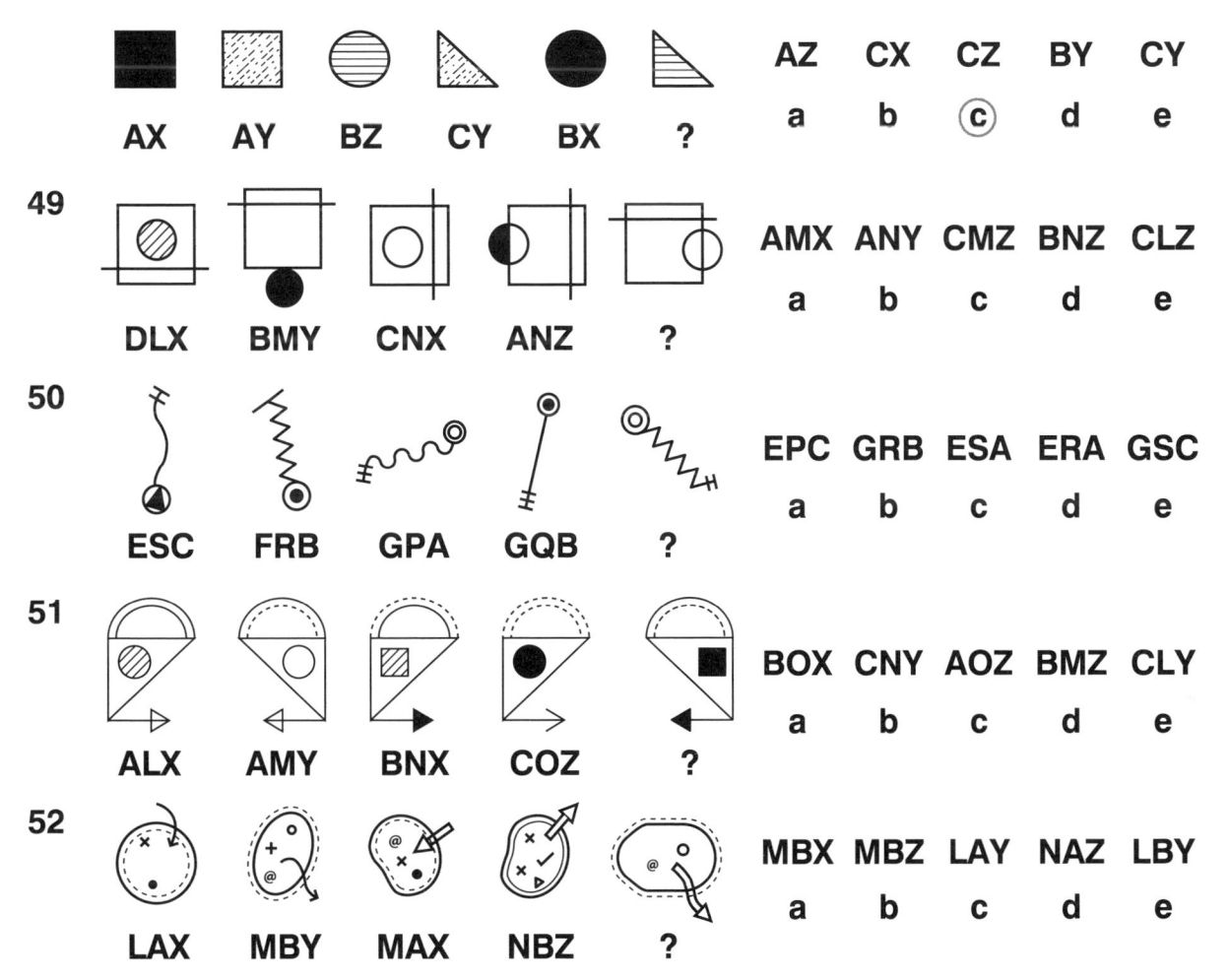

Example

	AZ	CX	CZ	BY	CY
	a	b	(c)	d	e

AX AY BZ CY BX ?

49

DLX BMY CNX ANZ ?

AMX	ANY	CMZ	BNZ	CLZ
a	b	c	d	e

50

ESC FRB GPA GQB ?

EPC	GRB	ESA	ERA	GSC
a	b	c	d	e

51

ALX AMY BNX COZ ?

BOX	CNY	AOZ	BMZ	CLY
a	b	c	d	e

52

LAX MBY MAX NBZ ?

MBX	MBZ	LAY	NAZ	LBY
a	b	c	d	e

53

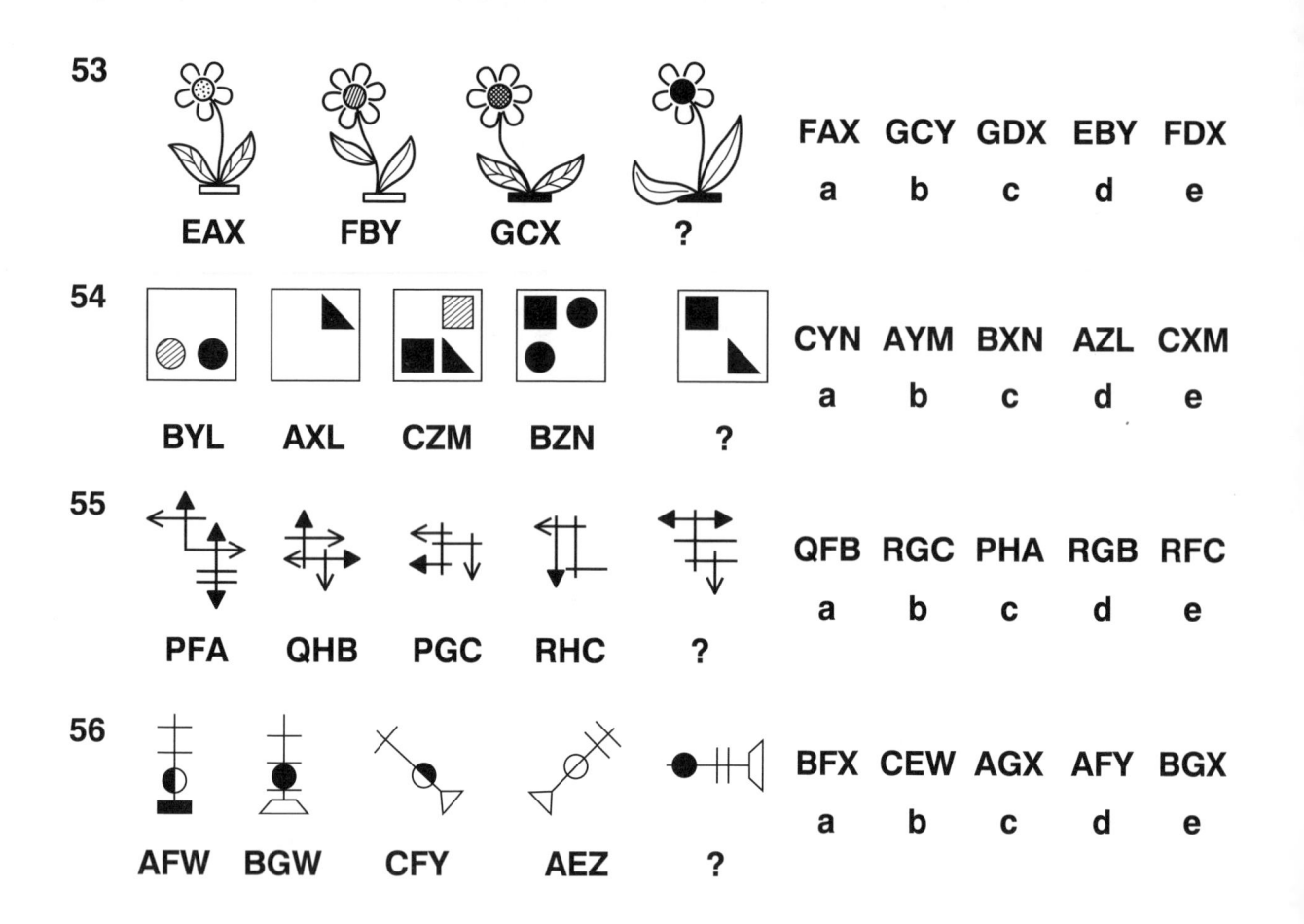

EAX FBY GCX ?

FAX	GCY	GDX	EBY	FDX
a	b	c	d	e

54

BYL AXL CZM BZN ?

CYN	AYM	BXN	AZL	CXM
a	b	c	d	e

55

PFA QHB PGC RHC ?

QFB	RGC	PHA	RGB	RFC
a	b	c	d	e

56

AFW BGW CFY AEZ ?

BFX	CEW	AGX	AFY	BGX
a	b	c	d	e

Which pattern on the right is formed by combining the two shapes on the left? Circle the letter.

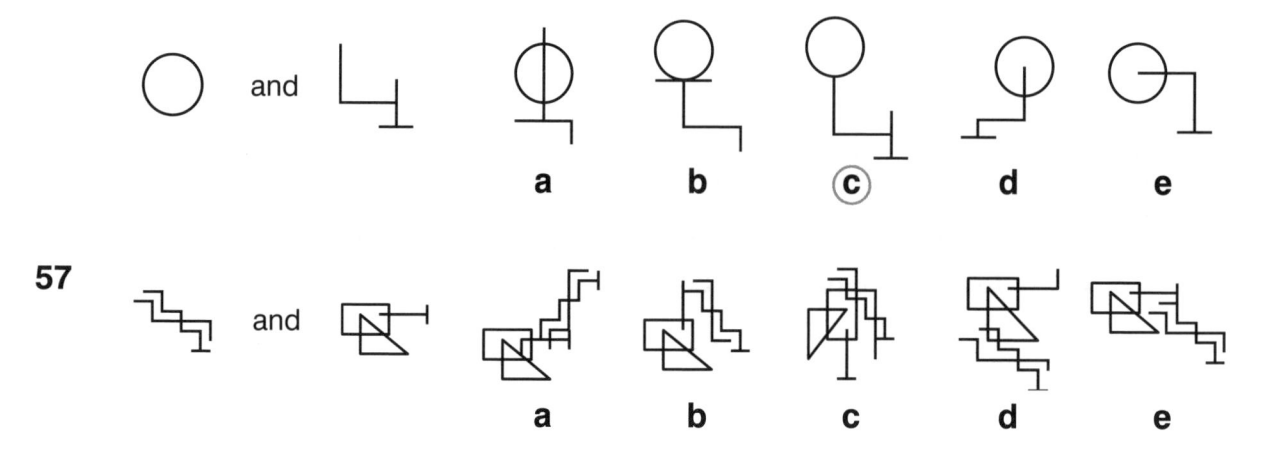

Example

○ and ⌐ a b **(c)** d e

57

a b c d e

58

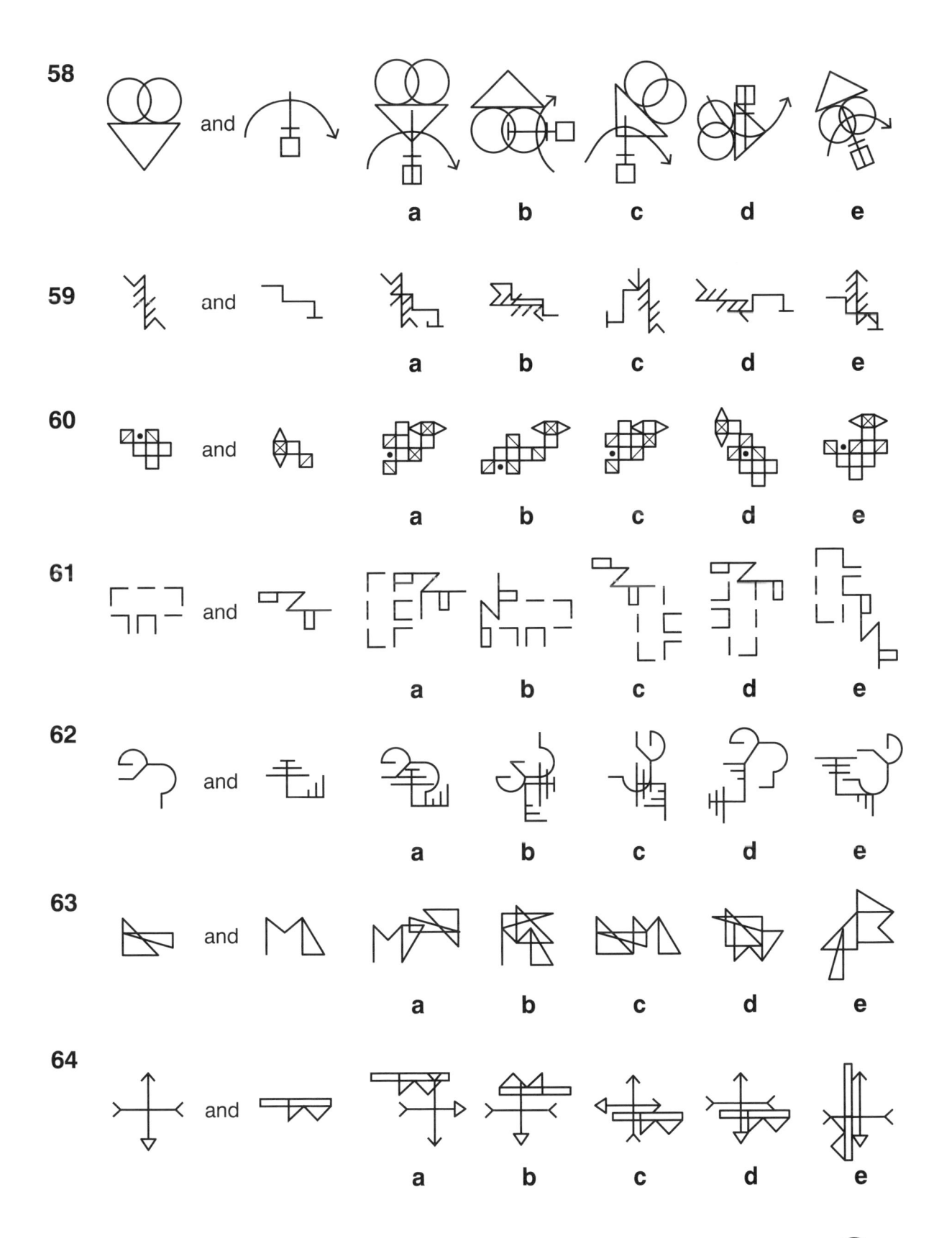

59

60

61

62

63

64

Mixed paper 2

Which of the shapes belongs to the group on the left? Circle the letter.

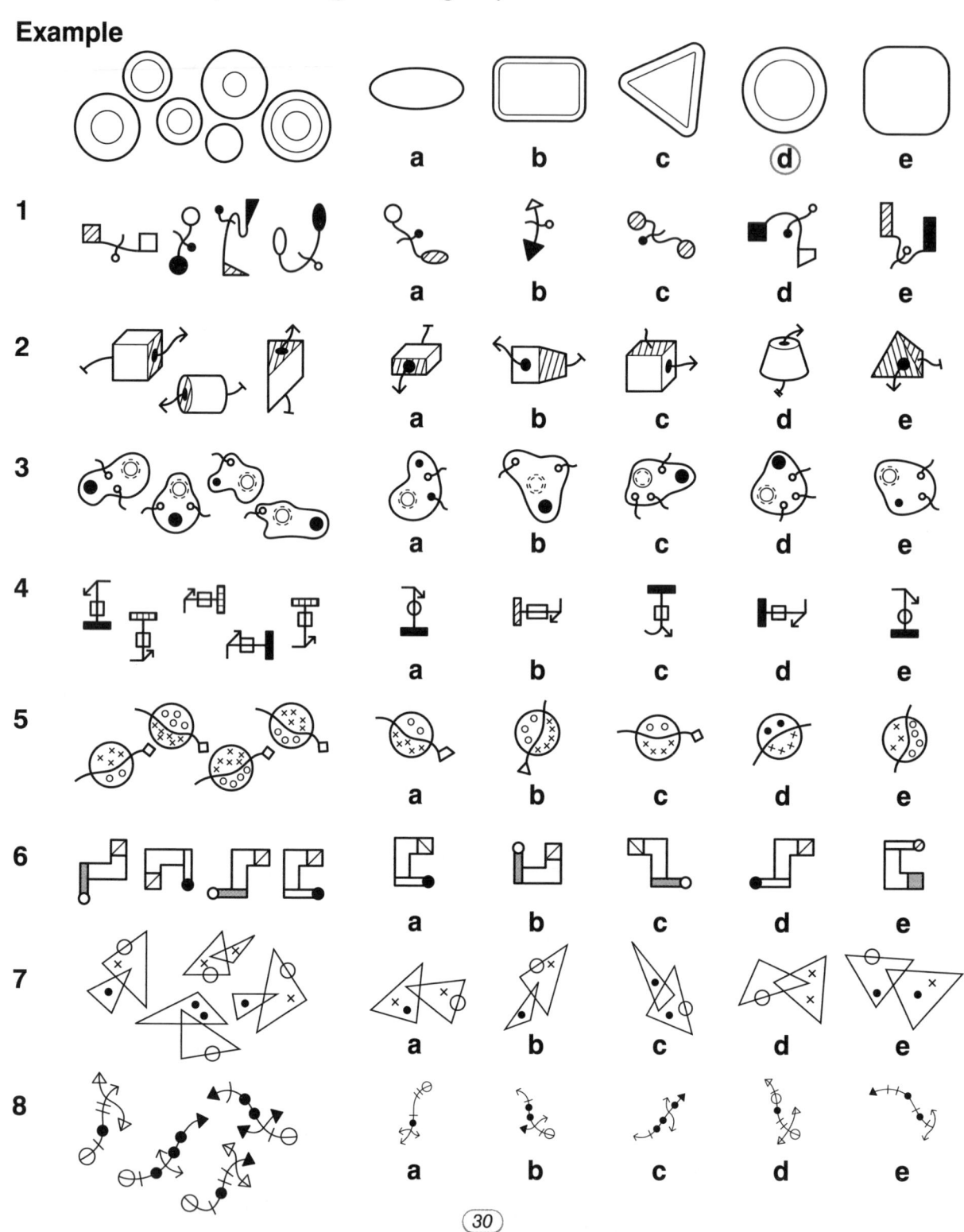

Example

a   b   c   (d)   e

1   a   b   c   d   e

2   a   b   c   d   e

3   a   b   c   d   e

4   a   b   c   d   e

5   a   b   c   d   e

6   a   b   c   d   e

7   a   b   c   d   e

8   a   b   c   d   e

Focus test 1: Similarities (pages 4–5)

1. **e** All of the shapes on the left have a triangle, which may be on the line or inside the square; the black circle is inside the square when the white circle overlaps the square's outline and outside the square when the white circle is inside the square.
2. **e** All of the shapes on the left have three zigzags, three circles and then a simple arrowhead in that order along a curvy line.
3. **a** All of the shapes on the left have a ring of five small circles, with two black arrowheads pointing to two adjacent circles and a circle on a short straight line extending from the circle opposite the arrows.
4. **d** All of the shapes on the left have a corner of a square and a corner of a triangle touching the edge of a circle; the circle has a smaller dotted circle within it, the square has a circle with a solid line within it and the triangle has a smaller triangle with a solid line within it.
5. **e** All of the shapes on the left have a circle with a downward pointing arrow from the bottom edge, a V-shaped line projects into the circle with a short line across one end of the V and a black spot at the other. The angle of the V is approximately 45°.
6. **c** All of the patterns on the left have a quadrilateral with a small black circle on the outside of one corner and a triangle adjacent to one side; a wavy line crosses the pattern, making a loop within the quadrilateral.
7. **c** All of the shapes on the left have five short lines radiating from one point; one of the lines ends in two small circles, first white and then black; another line has a short straight line across it.
8. **d** All of the patterns on the left are made up of five identically sized shapes with two of the diagonally opposite ones shaded black.
9. **b** All of the circles on the left have one white quarter, one black quarter, on quarter shaded with straight lines and one quarter shaded with cross-hatching; there is a small white circle touching the outside of the cross-hatched quarter and a small black circle touching the outside of the white quarter.
10. **e** All of the shapes on the left have a narrow, curved segment along the outside of one of the straight edges and an inner white circle touching the inside of that edge; there is a dotted line on the outside of one of the other straight edges.
11. **a** All of the patterns on the left have two triangles on either side of a circle, arranged so that the triangles are both pointing away from the circle; the curved line has an arrowhead each end.
12. **c** All of the shapes on the left have a thick black line with a double-ended arrow across it and a curved line across it with a black circle one end and a white circle the other; there is a curly tail at one end of the thick line and a short straight line at various positions.

Focus test 2: Grids (pages 6–7)

1. **e** The missing square will be a 90° clockwise rotation of the square above it.

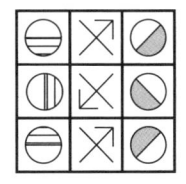

2. **b** The missing square will contain two triangles at bottom left, the first white and the second black.

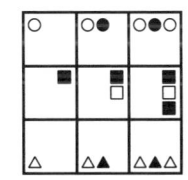

3. **d** The missing square is a 180° rotation of the first square in the second row.

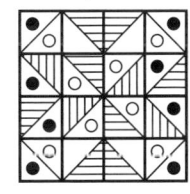

4. **c** The missing square will be a 45° clockwise rotation of the second square in the same row, with grey shading.

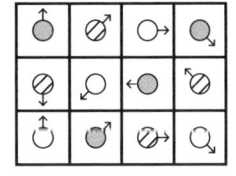

5. **e** The missing square will be the same as the second square in the second row.

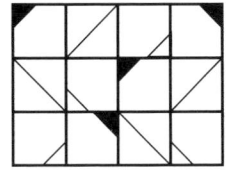

6 **a** The missing square will be shaded with cross-hatching, to match the adjacent small shape in the central square.

7 **e** The missing square will contain the white circle from the top triangle.

8 **d** The missing triangle will be a 120° clockwise rotation of the top triangle.

9 **e** The missing square will contain a small triangle as in the top triangle of the central square, and its reflection; the bottom half will be shaded with horizontal lines.

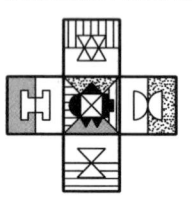

10 **c** The missing triangle will be the same at the top left and top right triangles, but with two small circles in the bottom section.

11 **d** The missing square will have an arrow in the bottom-right corner, with a white arrowhead; the white rectangle will be at the bottom of the square.

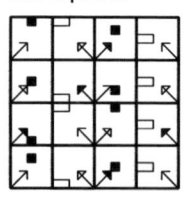

12 **b** The missing square will have a grey shaded square at bottom left, with a small triangle bottom right.

Focus test 3: Analogies (pages 8–9)

1 **d** To form the second shape, the grey shading changes to cross-hatching, the black circle in a white ring becomes a white circle in a black ring and the diagonal lines flip to create two triangles rather than one.

2 **c** The second shape is a 90° clockwise rotation of the first shape; the squares at the end of each rectangle swap their shading.

3 **d** The second shape is a 90° anticlockwise rotation of the first shape; the curved lines have become wide V-shapes; an additional white rectangle has been added underneath the existing two.

4 **d** The second shape is a 45° clockwise rotation of the first shape; the small black shape within the white shape has been enlarged and now surrounds the white shape; the angle in the arrow has been increased to 90° and the tail line has been doubled.

5 **e** To form the second shape, the dividing lines between the shapes has been removed, with the 'opposite sides' left in line; the whole shape keeps the same orientation and number of elements.

6 **b** The squares in the first shape have become circles in the second shape, on a curved line with a small circle at each end; these small circles have the same shading as the second square from the top. One of the larger circles has the same shading as the top square in the first shape; the other three circles have the same shading as the third square.

7 **e** To form the second shape, the three bars have been rotated 90° and set side by side; the shading of the central bar has been exchanged with the shading of the outer two bars; a fourth bar has been added, at right angles to the set of three, with the same shading as the original central bar.

8 **e** To form the second shape, the circles have become triangles and the triangles have become circles; shapes shaded black have become white and shapes shaded white have become black.

9 **d** To form the second shape, the grey shaded triangle has moved across to the other half of its small square area; the overlapping shapes have changed into a row of the same shape, the same number but smaller; the patterned band has moved to the other side of its small square area.

10 **c** To form the second shape, the circular line has become a straight line; the small central black shapes have become white and moved to either end of the line; the circles have been replaced by a wavy line that cuts across the straight line the same number of times as there were circles in the first shape on the original curve; the wavy line has the same arrowheads as the circular line in the first shape.

11 **e** The second shape is a 90° anticlockwise rotation of the first shape; the small white shape inside the black shape has moved to the other end of the central line; the straight lines have become curved lines across the straight line, before the end shape.

12 **a** The second shape is a 180° rotation of the first shape; the small black shapes have moved out of the small squares and lines now join them to the centre of their squares; the shading of the larger shape has changed from diagonal lines to cross-hatching.

Focus test 4: Reflections (pages 10–11)

1–12 When each shape is paired with the correct reflection, they form a single shape that is perfectly symmetrical.

1 **d**

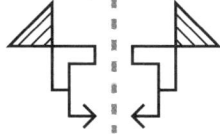

2 **e**

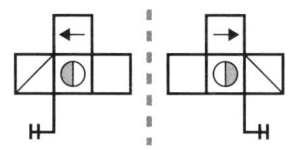

3 **e**

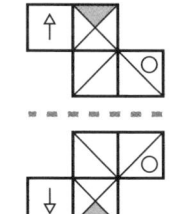

4 **c**

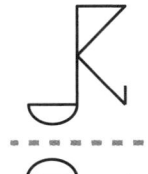

5 **e**

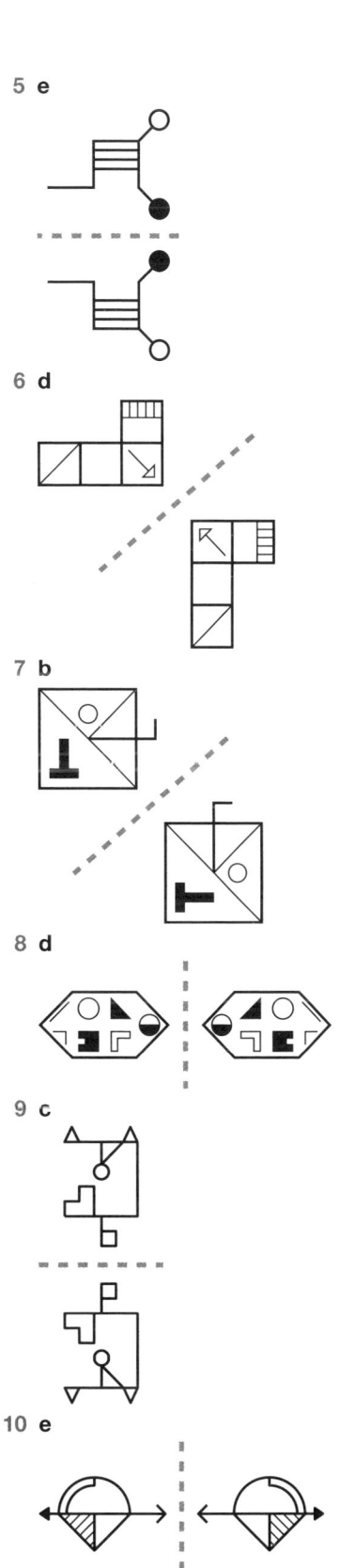

6 **d**

7 **b**

8 **d**

9 **c**

10 **e**

11 c

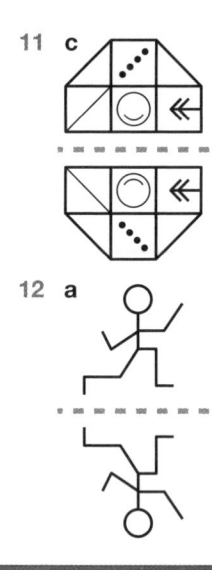

12 a

Focus test 5: Sequences (pages 12–13)

1. **c** The black spot moves down the diagonal line; the base line follows a repeating pattern of –left–T-shape–right; the white square alternates between right and left.
2. **c** There are two alternating sequences: the first, third, fifth (and so on) shapes have two overlapping circles of different sizes, with the overlapping section shaded grey; the large circle alternates between the top and bottom position; there is an increasing number of small white circles inside the large circle.
3. **e** The white shapes follow a repeating pattern of –triangle–circle–square–; the triangles alternate between pointing up and pointing down; the arrow at the base of the Z-line rotates 90° clockwise each time.
4. **d** The short line at the top of the shape alternates between the left and right; the number of short horizontal lines across the centre alternates between three and one; the sequence of patterns inside the circle is –cross–white–grey–.
5. **a** The number of squares in the diagonal increases by one each time; the circles within them alternate between black and white; the arrow in the top cross rotates 90° clockwise; at the base, IX alternates with XI.
6. **e** The number of short lines at the top alternates between three and one; the white shape follows the sequence –circle–diamond–square–; the black shape at the bottom follows the sequence –square–circle–diamond–.
7. **e** The number of short lines at the top of the shape count up from one to three and then back down to one again, and so on; the arrowhead at the base alternates between white and black.
8. **d** The top bar alternates between black and white; the short horizontal lines at the base increase by one each time and are added alternately to the left side and then the right; there are always four circles – there is no pattern governing the position of the black one.
9. **b** The circles alternate between black and white, with the number increasing by one after each pair; there are always three small rectangles to the right and the diagonal line in the bottom rectangle alternates.
10. **d** The arrowheads alternate between white and black; the short line at the base with a black spot moves like a pendulum, swinging 45° each time first to the right until horizontal and then to the left.
11. **e** The straight line alternates between a horizontal and a vertical position; the dot at the (left/top) end of the line alternates between black and white; the number of short lines across the other end decreases by one every second shape; the number of arrow tails on the curved arrow increases by one every second shape.
12. **d** The head of the 'pin' shape projecting into the loop alternates between black and white; the number of white circles inside the loop increases by one each time; there are always two crosses inside the loop.

Focus test 6: Cubes (pages 14–15)

1. **e** When the four triangles are on the front of the cube, with the grey one at the top, and the circle on the right, the parallel lines will be on the top face, but they will be horizontal, not vertical.
2. **c** The arrow points at the triangle, not the diagonal line.
3. **d** The double-ended arrow points at the plain circle, so cannot be parallel to it.
4. **e** The two arrows do not both point into the same corner.
5. **c** The grey bar and the L-shape are in opposite positions, so they cannot therefore be seen as adjacent faces on the cube.
6. **e** The face with the black and one of the L-shapes are in opposite positions, so the face with the black spot cannot be adjacent to both of the L-shapes.
7. **a** When the face with the black spot is on the front of the cube, with the @ symbol on the right, the parallel lines will be on the right face, but they will be horizontal, not vertical.

8 **a** In the face adjacent to the bottom of the T-shape, the parallel lines are parallel to the top bar of the T, not perpendicular to it.

9 **d** The triangle points at the arrow, not the circle.

10 **a** If the pentagon is positioned in this way, the filled black circle must be on the right face.

11 **b** The diameter of the half-shaded circle is parallel to the edges of the square, not on the diagonal.

12 **c** The triangle and the L-shape are in opposite positions, so they cannot therefore be seen as adjacent faces on the cube.

Focus test 7: Codes (pages 16–17)

1 **d** The first letter represents the shading of the square (A has vertical/horizontal cross-hatching, B has solid black shading, C has diagonal cross-hatching and D has horizontal lines). The second letter represents the position of the triangle in relation to the square (W has the triangle below the square, Y has the triangle above and Z has the triangle on the left, so by deduction X has the triangle on the right of the square).

2 **b** The first letter represents the angle of the line (A has the line pointing straight up, B has it pointing straight down, C has it pointing to the left and E has it on the diagonal to bottom left, so by deduction D has it on the diagonal to top right). The second letter represents the number of circles (X has one circle, Y has two and Z has three).

3 **b** The first letter represents the shading of the triangle (A has solid black shading, B has horizontal lines, C has diagonal lines and D has cross-hatching). The second letter represents the side of the square from which the triangle projects (L has the triangle bottom right, N has it top left and P has it top right, so by deduction M has the triangle bottom left).

4 **d** The first letter represents the number of thin white rectangles (A has two rectangles, B has three and C has four). The second letter represents the orientation of the rectangles (L has them horizontal and M has them vertical). The third letter represents the direction of the lines projecting from the shape (Y has the two lines projecting in opposite directions and Z has both lines projecting in the same direction).

5 **c** The first letter represents the number of short horizontal lines (A has one short horizontal line, B has two and C has three). The second letter represents the position of the small square in the large one (E has the small square bottom left, F has it bottom right and G has it top right, so by deduction H has the small square top left. The third letter represents the position of the thin rectangle along the edge of the square (S has the rectangle at the bottom and T has it at the top).

6 **a** The first letter represents the position in the whole shape of the straight line without the triangle (D has it on the left, E has it at the top and G has it along the bottom, so by deduction F has it on the right). The second letter represents the shading and position of the triangle in relation to the two lines (P has a white triangle within the angle made by the two lines, Q has a black triangle within the angle, R has a white triangle on the outside of the lines and S has a black triangle on the outside of the lines).

7 **e** The first letter represents the colour of the circle (A has a black circle and B has a white circle). The second letter represents the direction of the three parallel lines (E has the three lines projecting to the right (east), N has them projecting to the top (north), W has them projecting to the left (west) and S has them projecting to the bottom (south)). The third letter represents the length of line to which the circle is attached (X has the circle on the longest of the three lines and Z has the circle on the shortest).

8 **d** The first letter represents the shading of the top right square (A has solid black shading, B has cross-hatching, C has dots and D is white, so by deduction E has diagonal lines). The second letter represents the number of white squares in the shape (X has three white squares, Y has one and Z has two).

9 **e** The first letter represents the arrow style and position (A has a double-headed with both ends outside the loop, B has a single-headed arrow ending inside the loop and C has a double-headed arrow with one end inside the loop). The second letter represents the shading of the small circle (E has a single line inside the circle, F has solid white shading, G has cross-hatching and H has solid black shading). The third letter represents the white shape across the outline (K has a circle, L has a triangle and M has a rectangle).

10 **c** The first letter represents the shading of the square (A has solid white shading, B has a cross inside the square, C has cross-hatching and D has solid black shading). The second letter represents the position of the circle (S

has the circle crossing a side of the triangle and T has it across one of the corners of the triangle). The third letter represents the shape and position of the black shaded part of the circle (Z has a semicircle inside the triangle shaded black, Y has a semicircle outside the triangle shaded black and W has the large section of the circle outside the triangle shaded black, so by deduction X has the small section of the circle inside the triangle shaded black).

11 **d** The first letter represents the pattern at the top end of the shape (A has a small white triangle, B has a dark zigzag pattern and C has short straight lines). The second letter represents the number of dots in the line (L has five dots, M has four and N has three). The third letter represents the shape at the lower end of the shape (Q has a small circle, R has a diamond, S has a large circle and T has a square).

12 **d** The first letter represents the direction of the black-headed arrow (A has it pointing to the top, B has it pointing to the right and C has it pointing to the bottom, so by deduction D has the arrow pointing to the left). The second letter represents the compass point the plain arrow points away from (S means it points to the North, W points to the East, N points South and E has it pointing to the West). The third letter represents the number of short lines crossing the diagonal line (L has two lines and O has three).

Focus test 8: Combining Shapes
(pages 18–19)

1 **d** The first shape has been rotated 90° anticlockwise.

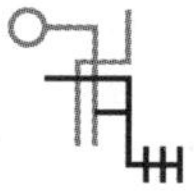

2 **a** The first shape has been rotated 90° clockwise.

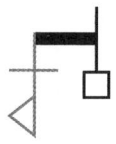

3 **b** The first shape has been rotated 90° clockwise.

4 **d** The second shape has been rotated 90° clockwise.

5 **c** Both shapes have been rotated 90° anticlockwise.

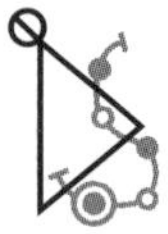

6 **c** The first shape has been rotated 90° clockwise. The second shape has been rotated 180°.

7 **d** The first shape has been rotated 90° clockwise. The second shape has been rotated 90° anticlockwise.

8 **e** Both shapes have been rotated 90° clockwise.

9 **b** Neither shape has been rotated, they are overlapping.

10 **c** The first shape has been rotated 180°.

11 **a** Neither shape has been rotated, they are overlapping.

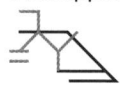

12 **c** The second shape has been rotated 180°.

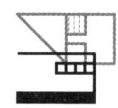

Mixed paper 1 (pages 20–29)

1 **e** All of the right-angled triangles on the left have sides of different lengths, a short arrow across the short side and a circle touching the outside of the hypotenuse.

2 **d** All of the shapes on the left have two squares of different sizes, with one black dot in the smaller square and one white circle in the larger square.

3 **a** All of the joined lines on the left have a dashed line for one of the long sides, with a small black circle at its end. A short arrow points inwards across the short side and another points outwards across the solid line long side; there is a small square in the corner where the two solid lines meet.

4 **c** All of the shapes on the left have the same number of loops as black spots; a simple arrow extends from the black square across the width of the rectangle and across the long side. Option b has the wrong arrowhead.

5 **d** All of the ovals on the left have a coiled line that joins a wavy line across the oval at a black spot; there is a small white circle beyond the wavy line which has one diagonal line across it.

6 **e** All of the shapes on the left have an outline that forms two loops; there is a circle overlapping the outline between the two loops; on the outline outside the loops there are two V-shapes crossing the line, one pointing inside the shape and one pointing outside; also outside the loops, two short straight lines cross the line.

7 **e** All of the shapes on the left have four sections of outline: one with a solid line, one with a dotted line and two with a double line (a pair of solid lines and a dashed line paired with a solid line); the two double lines are opposite each other in the shape; the double solid line is curved.

8 **d** All of the triangles on the left have a mixture of black and white circles and squares outside their corners; when the triangle touches a square, it is at the mid-point of one side of the square.

9 **b** The missing square will contain the shape at the top of the third square in the middle row, positioned at the bottom of the square.

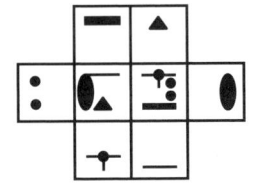

10 **e** The pattern of squares, lines and dots in the top row is reflected and repeated in the bottom row, ignoring the black triangles.

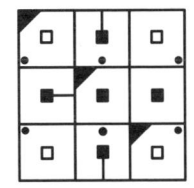

11 **d** The missing square must have a white circle in the top-left corner to complete the pattern of small circles. The longest stripe in the triangle must be white.

12 **e** The missing square will be a horizontal reflection of the arrow in the square directly above it, except that the small black-and-white square will be rotated so that the white half is at the top.

13 **c** The shading of the crescent shapes follows a repeating pattern of black–lined–white progressively along one row then back along the row underneath so the correct answer will be lined. Across each row, the small shape moves to the next corner in a clockwise rotation so the correct answer needs a square top-left.

14 **d** The missing square will contain a triangle with diagonal cross-hatch shading to the bottom-left (because the pattern rotates through 45°) and a circle with a cross in it so there are two with each shading overall.

15 e The triangles are in reflected pairs. The missing triangle will be a vertical reflection of the last triangle.

16 d The small shapes in the central square are the same as the larger shape in one of the adjacent outer squares and take the shading style of the other adjacent outer square. The shading of the triangle in the inner squares is the same as the opposite outer square. The missing square will have the bottom-right triangular half shaded with dots and a small square with diagonal cross-hatching.

17 d To form the second pattern, the two 2-D shapes on the left-hand side of the central vertical line have swapped places, as have the two 2-D shape on the right-hand side of the line; the lines projecting from the vertical line have rotated 180°.

18 c The second pattern is two vertical reflections of the first shape; in the left-hand reflection the shading lines in the bottom square have also been rotated by 90°; in the right-hand reflection the shading in the squares has been removed.

19 a The second pattern is made from the 2-D shapes in the first pattern, resized and drawn concentric with the outermost band shaded black. The arrow is now straight, with a smaller arrowhead; it has the same number of lines on its tail as in the first shape. The arrow in the new shape points down but to the opposite side to the original.

20 e The second pattern is formed using all the elements of the first pattern, with the straight lines and part shapes arranged alternately around the single complete shape, without touching.

21 d The second pattern is formed by doubling the single right-angle line and adding a black square in the open corner; the diagonal lines have rotated 135° clockwise to become vertical and the half arrowheads have become T-line endings.

22 c The second large shape is a vertical reflection of the first shape; the white ovals have become black circles; the cross inside the inner circle has been replaced with a black/white semicircle with the black half closest to the small black circles.

23 e The second shape is formed by combining the bottom-left and top-right quarters of the first shape.

24 c The second shape is formed by combining the top two rectangles into a bottom row; a long rectangle above them contains the same number of black spots as there are crosses in the first shape.

25–32 When each shape is paired with the correct reflection, they form a single shape that is perfectly symmetrical.

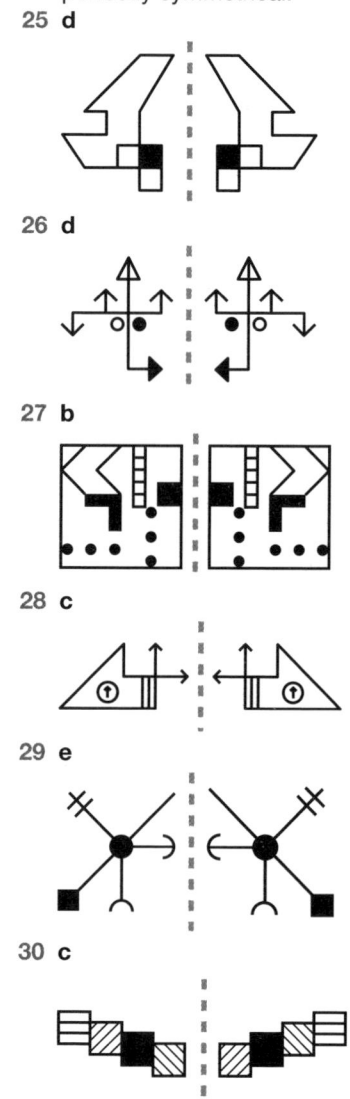

25 d

26 d

27 b

28 c

29 e

30 c

31 **e**

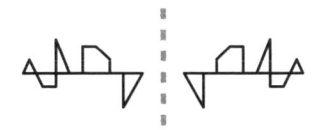

32 **d**

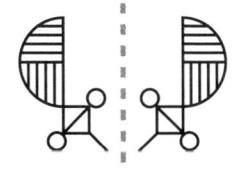

33 **d** The linked circles alternate between black and white, following the repeating sequence – three–two–one–; the short horizontal line moves down the shape, going from left to right then back again; the circles at the bottom right alternate position in the square, with two black then two white, and so on.

34 **e** The shape is the same as the second and fourth shapes, with the arrow alternating between pointing up or down; there are no clues about shading so option e is the best fit option.

35 **e** The line with the circle rotates 45° anticlockwise each time and alternates between long and short; the circle shading follows the repeating pattern –cross–white–black–; the line with the black triangle rotates 30° anticlockwise each time.

36 **a** Every second shape is a square. Looking just at the square, the arrow increases in length each time, crossing a different side of the square each time and going alternately into and out of the square, with the arrowhead always going down into the square at the top; the black square rotates 90° clockwise around the square; the white circle is constant at the bottom right corner.

37 **c** Horizontal and vertical lines are added alternately; the T-shape ending moves between the base and the top; the arrow alternates between pointing up and pointing down, progressively moving up the horizontal lines.

38 **d** This is a repeating pattern of five shapes. In the second instance, the inner shape moves below the main shape and there a double (solid) line along the part of the edge where the dotted line appears in the first shape.

39 **e** The position of the arrow alternates between the top and the bottom of the circle; the white circle rotates 90° clockwise around the perimeter; and the inner square rotates 90° anticlockwise each time.

40 **e** A new column of black dots is alternately added to the right and to the left of the squares; the larger square at the bottom rotates 90° clockwise each time; the short vertical line underneath the bottom square moves from left to right.

41 **b** When the black circle is on the front of the cube and the triangle on the right, the parallel lines will be on the top, but they will point towards the circle, not the triangle.

42 **e** The V points towards the L-shape, not the crescent.

43 **c** The L-shape and the black bar are in opposite positions, so they cannot therefore be seen as adjacent faces on the cube.

44 **a** When the two faces with the black triangles are adjacent, with the triangles at the top edge of the faces, the one with the white circle will be on the right of the other, not the left.

45 **a** The black half of the circle is adjacent to the triangle, not the arrowed shape.

46 **e** The four L-shapes are in a line in the net, so three of them cannot be seen as adjacent faces at a corner on the cube.

47 **d** One end of the double-headed arrow points at the corner of the L-shape, not one of its ends.

48 **c** The two black triangles are in opposite positions, so they cannot therefore be seen as adjacent faces on the cube.

49 **c** The first letter represents the shading of the circle (A has a half black, half white circles, B has a plain black circle, C has a plain white circle and D has a circle with diagonal line shading). The second letter represents the position of the line (L has the line across the bottom, M has the line across the top and N has the line down the right). The third letter represents the position of the circle in relation to the square (X has the circle inside the square, Y has it outside and Z has the circle overlapping the outline of the square).

50 **d** The first letter represents the number of short lines across the 'tail' (E has two lines, F has one and G has three). The second letter represents the style of the line (P has a line made from linked U-shapes, Q has a straight line, R has a zigzag line and S has a slightly wavy line). The third letter represents the style of the shape inside the white circle (A has a second white circle, B has a black circle and C has a black triangle).

51 **d** The first letter represents the style of the arrowhead at the base of the shape (A has a white arrowhead, B has a black arrowhead and C has a plain arrowhead). The second letter represents the style of the line used for the

semicircle at the top (L has a double solid line, M has a solid outer line with a dashed inner line dashed, N has a dashed outer line with a solid inner line and has a double dashed line). The third letter represents the shading of the shape inside the triangle (X has diagonal line shading, Y has plain white shading and Z has plain black shading).

52 **e** The first letter represents the number of small shapes inside the larger shape (L has two, M has three and N has four). The second letter represents the direction of the arrow (A has the arrow pointing into the shape and B has the arrow pointing out of the shape). The third letter represents the line style around the shape (X has a solid outer line with an inner dotted line, Y has a solid inner line with a dotted outer line and Z has a double solid line).

53 **e** The first letter represents the style of the line markings on the leaves (E has lines alternating between left and right of the central line, F has just the central line and G has lines in pairs from the central line). The second letter represents the shading in the middle of the flower (A has dots, B has diagonal lines and C has cross-hatching). The third letter represents the position of the leaves (X has both leaves joined to the stem at the base and Y has one leaf at the base and one higher up).

54 **b** The first letter represents the shape in the bottom-left corner of the square (A has no shape, B has a circle and C has a square). The second letter represents the total number of shapes within the square (X has one shape, Y has two and Z has three). The third letter represents the number of black shapes in the square (L has one black shape, M has two and N has three).

55 **d** The first letter represents the number of plain arrowheads (R has one plain arrowhead, P has two and Q has three). The second letter represents the number of lines or arrows (F has six lines or arrows, G has five and H has four). The third letter represents the number of black arrowheads (A has three black arrowhead, B has two and C has one).

56 **c** The first letter represents the number of short lines crossing the main line of the shape (A has two, B has three and C has one). The second letter represents the shading of the circle (E has a white circle, F has a half black, half white circle and G has a black circle). The third letter represents the orientation of the central line (W has a vertical line, Y has a diagonal line from top left to bottom right and Z has a diagonal line from bottom left to top right, so by deduction X has a horizontal line).

57 **e** There are three 'steps' in one of the lines in the first shape, and two in the other. The line in the second shape is parallel to the longer side of the rectangle and ends in a T-shape.

58 **c** The first shape has been rotated 45° clockwise.

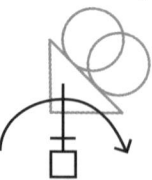

59 **c** The second shape has been rotated 90° clockwise.

60 **d** Neither shape has been rotated, they are positioned adjacent. The first shape has six squares, but more can be formed when it is put alongside the second shape.

61 **b** The second shape has been rotated 90° anticlockwise.

62 **a** Neither shape has been rotated, they are overlapping.

63 **c** Neither shape has been rotated, they are overlapping.

64 **d** The first shape consists of a double-headed arrow with one open and one closed arrowheads, and a line with inverted open arrowheads at each end. In the second shape, the section with the triangles underneath is more than half the width of the whole shape.

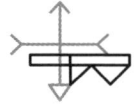

Mixed paper 2 (pages 29–39)

1 **e** All of the shapes on the left are made up of two identical shapes shaded differently, linked by a curved line across which there is a short, curved line with a black or white circle at the end.

2 **a** All of the shapes on the left are 3-D solids with a hole (black circle) in the middle of a diagonally lined shaded face; a simple arrow with a T-tail emerges through the hole from the far side of the solid.

3 **e** All of the shapes on the left have within them a circle with a plain line and an outer dashed line, a black circle of varying size and one or two small white circles with curved tails that go across the outline of the shape.

4 **d** All of the shapes of the left have a line perpendicular to a thin rectangular base with varying shading; the line passes through a square; at the top of the line an arrow points down at 45° and a short horizontal line sticks out in the opposite direction.

5 All of the circles on the left are divided by a wavy line, with fixed number of crosses on one side and small white circles on the other (4× = 2o; 6× = 4o; 5× = 3o). There is a small square at one end of the wavy line.

6 **c** All of the shapes are made up of an L-shape and a thin rectangular bar; when the bar is grey the configuration is as a Z; when the thin bar has a black head, the configuration is a U-shape. The diagonal line in the small square is in the opposite direction in option 'a'.

7 **b** All of the patterns on the left have two overlapping triangles; one of the triangles is right-angled, and a circle overlaps one of its shorter sides; there are two other elements – a cross and a black spot, or two of either.

8 **a** All of the patterns on the left have a long, curved line with a circle at one end and an arrow at the other; a short, curved arrow, with both ends the same style, crosses the main line; there are four other elements on the main line – a mixture of black circles and short straight lines.

9 **a** The missing square is a 90° clockwise rotation of the middle bottom square, with one small square added on the inside.

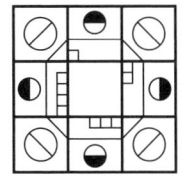

10 **c** There is a repeating pattern of 1, 2, 3 black dots so the missing square will have one black spot at the top. The square corner is in the same position along the first two rows and alternates from left to right along the third row so it must be on the right with a short diagonal line pointing inwards from the opposite (bottom-left) corner.

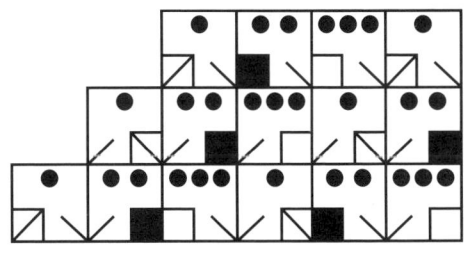

11 **e** The missing square will be a vertical reflection of the second square in the same row.

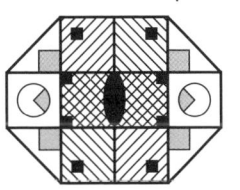

12 **d** The missing triangle will contain a black arrow angled down from the top, with no horizontal band; in the tip will be a large, shaded triangle and no circle. There is a pattern of the dashes starting from left in the top and right in the bottom triangles so there must be 2 dashes starting on the right hand side. The arrow heads alternate black or open between the top and bottom triangles so there must be a black arrow.

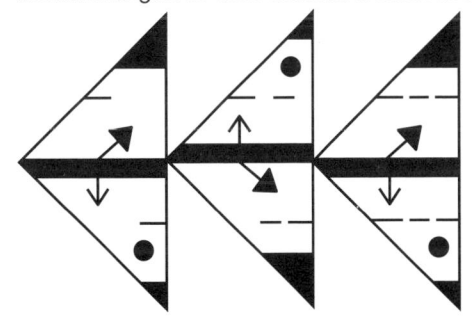

13 d The line at the outer edge of the square is the same style as the opposite side of the small central square so the missing square will contain a dashed vertical line at the right-hand side. The small shapes around the central square are copied into the outer square but swap places and, as the shading is different in each of the outer three squares, by deduction it must be a black circle and white square. Finally, a reflection of the arrow in the left-hand square in the middle.

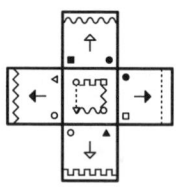

14 c The missing triangle will contain a vertical reflection of the corresponding triangle on the left of the shape, with the grey and white shading swapped.

15 b The missing triangle will be a horizontal reflection of the top triangle, except that there will be four short horizontal lines in the centre.

16 d The missing rectangle will have a black spot at the bottom, a cross in the middle and a curved arrow with a white arrowhead pointing up. The black spot alternates between the top and the bottom of the rectangles with a white circle alternating with the black spots; the cross moves down from top to middle to bottom along the top row and from the bottom to the top in the second row. The arrows follow the sequence of plain, white arrowhead, dotted line with a T-end, and they alternate pointing up or down within the rectangle.

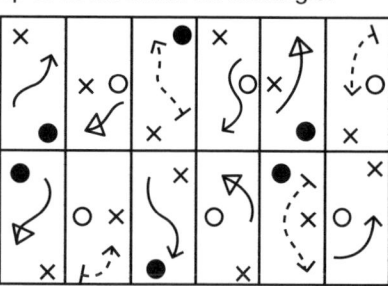

17 d The second shape is a horizontal reflection of the first shape, with the white and grey shading swapped.

18 e To form the second pattern, each small shape in the first pattern is seen twice within a loop shape; each pair of shapes overlap and the overlap is grey if the original shapes were grey in the first pattern; the number of wavy lines on the outline, and the number of times each crosses the outline, is determined by the number of shapes in the first pattern.

19 b The second shape is a 135° clockwise rotation of the first shape; dotted lines have become plain, double-ended arrows have become plain lines and plain lines have become double-ended arrows.

20 c To form the second shape, the pattern along the edge of the first square is rotated 90° clockwise and located in the bottom-left corner of a larger square; the two shapes are copied together, both shaded, in the bottom-right corner; the two shapes are also copied and separated, one to the left and one to the right in the upper half of the square.

21 b To form the second shape, the smaller shapes with tails have been arranged in a block; the black circles now become white circles with an inner black circle.

22 e To form the second pattern, each square in the first pattern has become a section of a circle; the black spots have become white circles; the black shape is repeated to match the number of squares in the first pattern.

23 c The second shape is a 90° clockwise rotation of the first shape; the small black shape has become white and the short straight lines have become arrowheads.

24 d There are the same number and colour of circles in the wavy shape as there are 'pins' in the regular shape, and the number of Vs gives the number of the other alternating circles, which have the shading of the central circle.

25–32 When each shape is paired with the correct reflection, they form a single shape that is perfectly symmetrical.

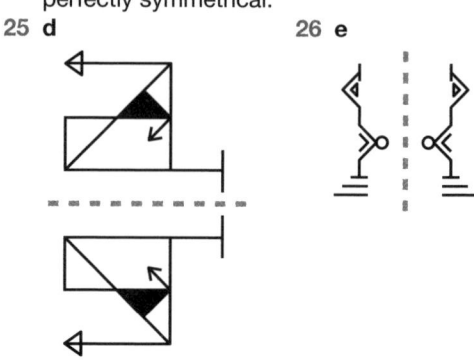

25 d **26 e**

27 c

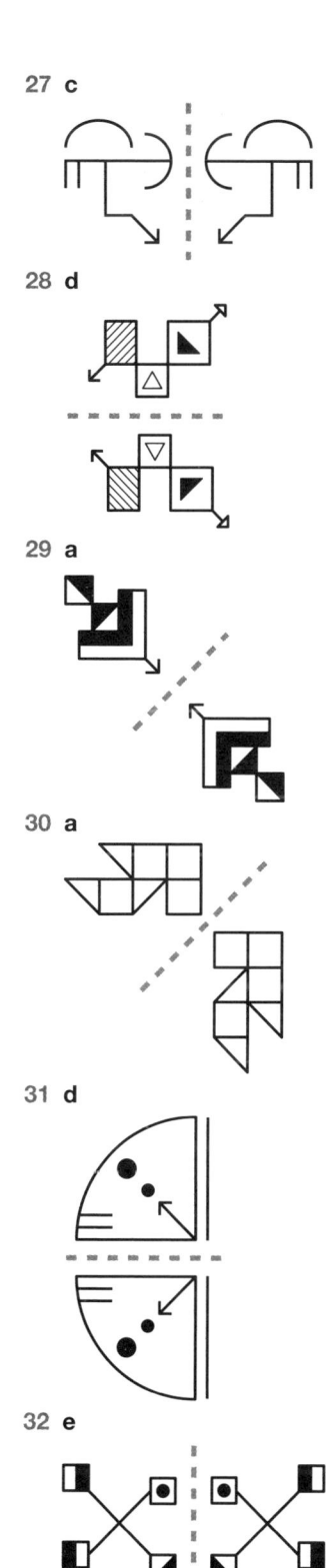

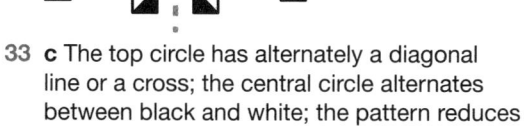

28 d

29 a

30 a

31 d

32 e

33 c The top circle has alternately a diagonal line or a cross; the central circle alternates between black and white; the pattern reduces by one circle each time.

34 d The L-shape in the squares rotates 90° clockwise each time; the small corner square with the diagonal also rotates by 90° clockwise and its inner triangle alternates between black and white.

35 e The shapes are alternately below the line, with white circles, and above the line, with black circles; the number of circles increases by one and the number of crosses decreases by one every second shape.

36 c The arrow in the larger circles rotates by 45° clockwise each time; the short, dashed line is always opposite the arrowhead within the circle; the small triangle on the outside alternates between the top and the bottom of the circle.

37 d There is a repeating pattern in the groups of three squares along the top row, with the shading of the circles changing from black to white and vice versa within each group of three.

38 c The diagonal line on the left moves from top to middle to bottom, then back to the top; dots are alternately added to the top and bottom of the column, making a column of alternate black and white dots; the vertical line on the right is alternately long and short and the style of ending on the line changes every two shapes.

39 b The shading in the square at the top right follows a repeating sequence of –diagonal (lower left to top right)–diagonal (top left to lower right)–cross–; the short horizontal line moves up the vertical line; and the horizontal U-shape moves up and down in three steps (–middle–top–middle–bottom–); the U-shape contains a repeating pattern of –black circle–white circle–nothing–.

40 b The line rotates 120° anticlockwise each time; the white circle moves 45° clockwise round the circle; the square alternates between right to left at the bottom and also rotates 90° clockwise each time.

41 c One end of the double-ended arrow points to the middle of one of the 'arms' of the L-shape, rather than being parallel to it.

42 e The cross-bar of the T-shape is parallel to the row of small squares, not perpendicular to it.

43 d The C-shape and V-shape both 'point' in the same direction, not towards each other.

44 b The right-angled arrow points towards the hypotenuse of the right-angle triangle, not one of the shorter sides.

45 e The two triangles are in opposition positions, so they cannot therefore be seen as adjacent faces on the cube.

46 **b** The arrow does not point in the same direction as either of the U-shapes.
47 **b** The two faces which are halved by diagonal lines both have a white half at their common edge.
48 **d** When the incomplete U-shape is on the top of the cube, in the orientation shown, the front face will be the face divided into quarters, not the one that is halved diagonally.
49 **d** The first letter represents the position of the white square (K has the white square at top left, L has it at top right and M has it at bottom right, so by deduction N has it at bottom left). The second letter represents the white shape within the large square (A has a triangle, B has a circle and C has a square). The third letter represents the shading of the small corner square (X has a black corner square, Y has a corner square with a cross and Z has a white corner square).
50 **c** The first letter represents the number and colour of the small circles (D has three black circle, E has three white and F has five white, so by deduction G has five black circles). The second letter represents the shading style within the 'shield' shapes (P has cross-hatching, Q has solid black shading). The third letter represents the orientation of the dividing line within the shield (X has a line dividing it vertically and Y has a line dividing it horizontally).
51 **e** The first letter represents the number of black circles (A has no black circles, B has one and C has two, so by deduction D has three). The second letter represents the orientation of the long rectangle (X has the long rectangle pointing to the left, Y has it pointing to the right and Z has it pointing up). The third letter represents the orientation of the right-angled triangle along the long edge (M has the hypotenuse nearest the triangular tip and N has a straight edge nearest the tip).
52 **c** The first letter represents the number of white circles (J has three white, K has four and L has five). The second letter represents the shading of the triangle (A has solid black shading in the inner section, B has solid black shading in the outer section, C has line shading in the outer section and D has line shading in the inner section). The third letter represents the number of short lines across the oval outline (X has one, Y has two and Z has three).
53 **e** The first letter represents the divisions of the large triangle (L has the triangle divided into two parts horizontally, M has the triangle divided into two parts vertically and N has the triangle divided into three parts with one

horizontal and one vertical line). The second letter represents the position of the white circle (A has the white circle at top left and C has it in the middle, so by deduction B has it at top right). The third letter represents the style of the line at the base tip of the triangle (T has a cross and R has an L-shape turning up, so by deduction S has an L-shape turning down).
54 **a** The first letter represents the style of the middle line (A has a dotted middle line and B has a dashed middle line, so by deduction C has a zigzag middle line). The second letter represents the style of the fourth line down (D has a plain line and E has a zigzag line). The third letter represents the style of the bottom line (X has a zigzag bottom line, Y has a dotted bottom line and Z has as plain bottom line).
55 **e** The first letter represents the style of the arrowhead (A has a plain arrowhead, B has a black arrowhead and C has a white arrowhead). The second letter represents the position of the dashed line (E has the dashed line as the inner part of the double line, F has the dashed line as the single side line, G has the dashed line as the outer part of the double line and H has the dashed line as the arrow line). The third letter represents the orientation of the corner of the L-shape (L has the corner at lower left, M has the corner at upper left and N has the corner at upper right, so by deduction O has the corner at lower right).
56 **b** The first letter represents the number of sides (D has five sides, E has six and F has seven). The second letter represents the number of white circles (A has one white circle and C has three, so by deduction B has two). The third letter represents the number of black circles (X has one black circle and Y has two, so by deduction Z has three).
57 **c** The first shape has been rotated 90° clockwise.
58 **c** The first shape has been rotated 90° anticlockwise.
59 **b** The first shape has been rotated 90° clockwise. The second shape has been rotated 180°.

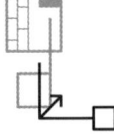

60 d The second shape has been rotated 180°.

61 b Neither shape has been rotated, they are overlapping.

62 e The first shape has been rotated 90° clockwise.

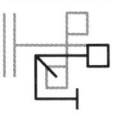

63 c Both shapes have been rotated 180°.

64 c The first shape has been rotated 90° clockwise.

Mixed paper 3 (pages 40–49)

1 **a** All of the shapes oWWthe left are symmetrical U-shapes with a plain line outside at the base of the U; when the U is formed with a simple solid line, there is a black circle inside it; when the U is formed with as an outline, there is a white circle within the outline.

2 **c** All of the L-shapes on the left have two different styles of arrowhead, one on each arm and touching the corner of the square which has a top-left to bottom-right diagonal. When the diagonal line starts at the corner touching the L-shape then one half of the square is shaded black.

3 **e** All of the shapes on the left have either a black circle on the line with an arrow that crosses the outline three times or a white circle on the line with an arrow that crosses the line twice.

4 **e** All of the shapes on the left have two concentric circles with the central circle shaded black or half black; a curved line runs from the centre to a small black circle outside which has three short lines projecting from it.

5 **a** All of the shapes on the left have a concentric triangle, square and circle (in any order); the triangle is always shaded.

6 **d** All of the cubes on the left have a total of seven spots visible, two of which are white.

7 **e** All of the shapes on the left have a black tip curving down; there is a pair of 'leaves', with both attached at the same point at the base of the shape.

8 **a** All of the shapes on the left are quadrilaterals with lines projecting from one side; the line styles are plain, zigzag, plain, dotted, in that order.

9 **d** The missing square will have a black circle in the centre, a short vertical line at bottom right and two short horizontal lines in the middle on the right.

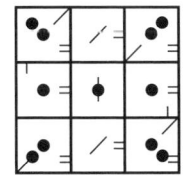

10 **c** The missing rectangle will have a cross-hatched square on the left, and the square on the right will have a T-shape at bottom left and a circle with a dot in it at top right.

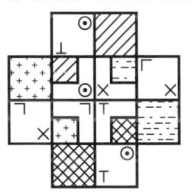

11 **d** The missing triangle will have line shading parallel to the hypotenuse; it will contain a black shape with three white spots in it; there will be three short lines at the end of the projecting line.

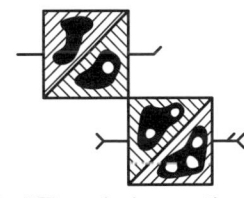

12 **d** The missing section will contain a grey rectangle, the same length as the rectangle in the top-right section.

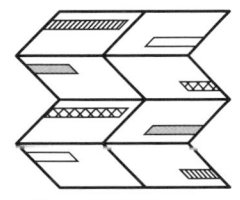

13 **e** There missing square will have the same black shape as the second square in the second row, with diagonal shading from top left to bottom right.

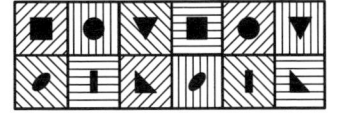

A15

14 b The missing square will contain the top small shapes from the bottom of the middle square in the top row, plus a black circle with a tail.

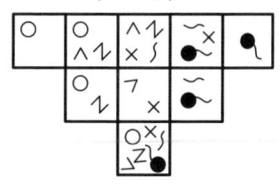

15 e The missing L-shape will be a vertical reflection of the L-shape on the left.

16 c The missing triangle will contain the same shape as the top-left triangle, with shading to match the top-right triangle.

17 d To form the second shape, each of the cubes in the bottom row of the first shape has become a circle; cubes with black top faces have become white circles and cubes with white top faces have become black circles.

18 e To form the second pattern, the two small shapes in the first pattern have swapped, with the black inner shape becoming the white shape and the white outer shape becoming the black inner shape; the number of side of the third, outer shape in the second pattern is determined by the number of horizontal lines in the first shape.

19 c To form the second pattern, each projection from the first shape has become a circle; the circles in the projections give the shading style of the end two circles; the central circle gives the shading style of the overlapping sections.

20 d To form the second pattern, the short lines projecting to the left of the vertical in the first pattern have become small triangles, the short lines crossing the vertical have become squares and the short lines projecting to the right of the vertical have become circles.

21 e To form the second pattern, the shapes projecting at the bottom of the sections with vertical shading have moved directly opposite to the top edge; the shading has been removed.

22 c To form the second shape, the first shape has been reflected above and then the whole double shape has been reflected to the right; in the right-hand half of the second shape, the black shading of the small squares has been replaced by black spots.

23 b To form the second pattern, the circles in the first pattern have become arrows pointing into a shape, with the colour of the arrowheads matching the colour of the circles; the number of sides of the large shape in the second pattern is determined by the number of times the curved line crosses the straight line in the first pattern.

24 c To form the second shape, the circles have rotated 180° and become squares; the shape in the lower circle has changed from black to white; the vertical line between the two circles and within the lower circle has changed, with a dashed line becoming solid and a solid line becoming dashed.

25–32 When each shape is paired with the correct reflection, they form a single shape that is perfectly symmetrical.

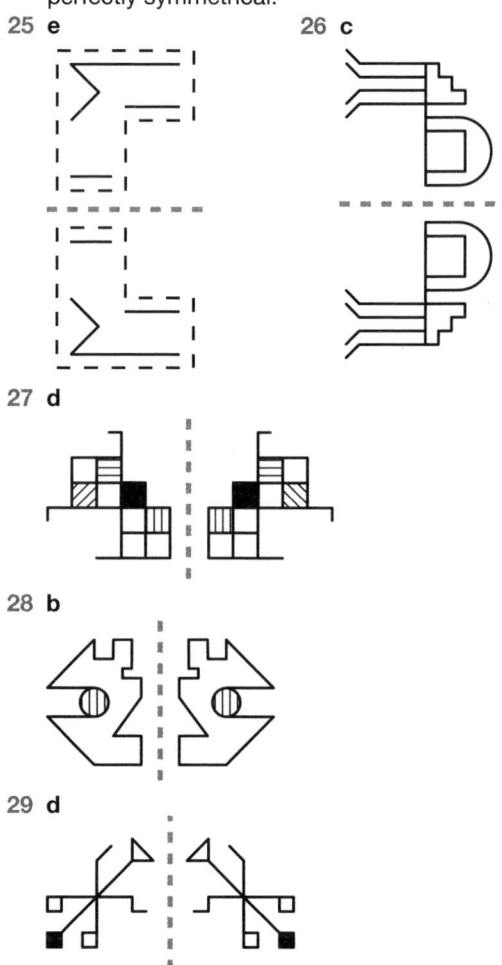

25 e

26 c

27 d

28 b

29 d

30 b

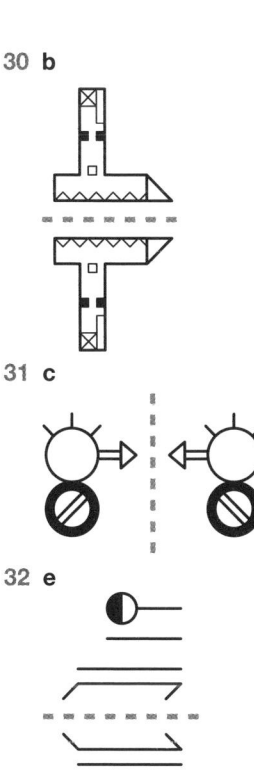

31 c

32 e

33 b The small shapes at the top follow the repeating pattern –square–circle–triangle–; the shapes and along the bottom follow the repeating pattern –right-angled triangle (with right-angle top-right)–right-angled triangle (with right angle top left)–equilateral triangle (with a straight edge at the top)–equilateral triangle (with a straight edge at the bottom)–; the shapes along the bottom have shading in the repeating pattern –white–black–vertical lines–; two black circles move progressively up the central column, starting again at the bottom when they reach the top.

34 e The cross moves from left to right across the top, the black spot moves down the right side and the number of small squares at the base alternates between two (one at each end) and one (in the middle).

35 a The arrow alternates between pointing down to the right and up to the right; the number of projections decreases each time, with a T-shape and a 'pin' shape removed alternately.

36 d The arms of the cross increase in length; the short diagonal lines alternate between pointing clockwise and anticlockwise; the centre alternates between a spot and a cross; the black squares are alternately on the vertical bars and the horizontal bars.

37 c The shape with the circle at the top alternates with the shape with the circle at the bottom, and in turn the direction of the lines from the top circle alternates between left and right.

38 b The main line rotates 90° clockwise each time; the short lines across the main line following a repeating pattern of –three–two–one–; the half-arrowhead is on one side for four shapes and then on the other side for the next four; the black circle is missing from every third shape.

39 e The total number of small shapes inside the circular shape decreases by one each time; the direction of the line at the top follows the repeating sequence of –diagonal (bottom left to top right)–vertical–diagonal (top left to bottom right)–horizontal–.

40 d The number of sides on the shape decreases by one each time; one small circle is added each time, alternating between black and white; the number of crosses follows the repeating pattern of –three–two–two–.

41 d When the parallel lines are on the top face of the cube and the L-shape on the front, the inverted U-shape will be on the left, not the two spots.

42 d The two line sections are parallel, not perpendicular, to the horizontal parts of the Z-shape.

43 c When the T-shape is on the top face of the cube and the small square is on the left, the L-shape is on the front, but its corner will be at top left, not top right.

44 c When the F-shape is on the front face of the cube, in the orientation shown, the arrow will be on the top, not a black bar.

45 e When the three bars are on the top face of the cube and the T-shape is on the front, the parallel lines will be on the left, but they will be perpendicular, not parallel, to the vertical in the T-shape.

46 c The equilateral triangle points to the double L-shape, not the C-shape.

47 d When the triangle is on the front and the face with the thick bar is on the top, the three bars will be on the right, but the three bars will be horizontal, not vertical.

48 b The edge shared between the face with the three black spots and the face with the half-shaded triangle and one black spot is along one side of the shaded triangle, not one of the white sides.

49 b The first letter represents the shape in the bottom-left corner (A has a circle in the bottom-left corner, B has a square, C has a triangle and D has a diamond). The second letter represents the shading of the circle (L has a white circle, M has a lined circle and N has a black circle). The third letter represents the direction of the arrow (Q has the arrow pointing to bottom left, R has it pointing to top left and S has it pointing to top right, so by deduction T has the arrow pointing to bottom right).

50 **c** The first letter represents the pair of spots (B has one black and one white spot and C has two black spots, so by deduction A has two white spots). The second letter represents the shading style of the lower rectangle in the middle (X has cross-hatching, Y has horizontal lines, Z has diagonal lines). The third letter represents the number of black rectangles (M has one black rectangle and N has two).

51 **e** The first letter represents the outermost shape of each pattern (P has a circle as the outermost shape and R has a square, so by deduction Q has a triangle as the outermost shape). The second letter represents the central shape (A has a circle as the central shape and B has a triangle, so by deduction C has a square as the central shape). The third letter represents the middle shape (X has a circle as the middle shape, Y has a triangle and Z has a square).

52 **c** The first letter represents the position of the horizontal side of the projecting triangular element at the top of the shape (A has the horizontal side lower left and B has the horizontal side upper left, so by deduction C has the horizontal side lower right). The second letter represents the position of the horizontal side of the projecting triangular element at the bottom of the shape (J has the horizontal side lower right, K has the horizontal side upper right and L has the horizontal side upper left). The third letter represents the pattern of the central stripes (R has a black stripe at the bottom and S has a black stripe in the centre, so by deduction T has a black stripe at the top).

53 **a** The first letter represents the number of black spots in the shape (A has one black spot, B has two and C has three). The second letter represents the number of short lines projecting from the circle (M has six short lines and N has five). The third letter represents the number of white circles with a cross in them (X has three white circles with a cross in, Y has two and Z has one).

54 **e** The first letter represents the configuration of the three circles (A has the three circles in a horizontal line, B has them in a triangular formation and C has them in a diagonal line from bottom left to top right, so by deduction D has the three circles in a diagonal line from top left to bottom right). The second letter represents the style of the vertical line (G has a thick straight black line, H has a thin straight line and J has a curved double line). The third letter represents the style of the base (P has a straight white base, Q has a straight black base, R has a straight white base with a dashed outline and S has a white curved base).

55 **a** The first letter represents the shading of the small square (L has a cross in it and M has solid black shading). The second letter represents the pattern of black and white circles along the base (A has all black circles and B has alternate white and black circles, so by deduction C has white–black–black–white). The third letter represents the style of the line across the top (R has a zigzag line, S has square battlements and T has triangular battlements).

56 **c** The first letter represents the number and orientation of the 'loops' (E has two loops on the left, F has three loops on the left, G has two loops on the right and H has three loops on the right). The second letter represents the shading of the circles (A has black circles and B has white. The third letter represents the orientation of the string circles (L has a horizontal string of circles and M has a vertical string of circles).

57 **d** The first shape has been rotated 180°. The second shape has been rotated 90°.

58 **e** Neither shape has been rotated, they are overlapping.

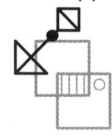

59 **c** The first shape has been rotated 90° anticlockwise. The second shape has been rotated 90° clockwise.

60 **a** The first shape has been rotated 90° anticlockwise.

61 **d** The first shape has been rotated 180°. The second shape has been rotated 90° anticlockwise.

62 **e** The first shape has been rotated 180°. The second shape has been rotated 90° clockwise.

63 **b** The first shape has been rotated 90° clockwise.

64 **e** The first shape has been rotated 90° clockwise.

Mixed paper 4 (pages 50–59)

1 **d** All of the curved lines on the left have two short straight lines across them; there is either a double arrowhead pointing towards a black spot or a single arrowhead pointing towards a white triangle; the curves with a white triangle have a white circle at the other end.

2 **a** All of the L-shapes on the left have one short curvy line across the short arm of the L, and two of different lengths across the long arm of the L, with the longer curved line nearer the top of the L.

3 **c** All of the shapes on the left have a right-angled triangle outside the square with the hypotenuse side touching a corner; this corner is either between two diagonally opposite corners containing black squares or diagonally opposite to and adjacent to two corners containing a white square; inside one of the black squares is a white circle, and inside one of the white squares is a black circle.

4 **d** All of the circles on the left are either divided into half, with two white circles projecting on two lines, or they are divided into quarters with two white quarters opposite each other, and with four white circles projecting on two lines.

5 **e** All of the right-angled triangles on the left have a small triangle across the hypotenuse; there is a circle across one of the shorter sides, with the inner section black; there is a square across the third side, with either the inner or the outer section black.

6 **a** All of the shapes on the left have a V-shape with an extra line along the outside of one 'arm'; the other 'arm' connects to the middle of one side of a square; there is a circle in the middle of the V; the square and the circle have different shading styles.

7 **c** All of the shapes on the left are reversed L-shapes with (when orientated as a reversed L) a small square at the top and three lines of increasing length projecting on the left, parallel to the base line of the L; the line below the square extends across the vertical and turns down, and the line above the bottom line has two dots at the end of it.

8 **d** All of the shapes on the left are like open boxes, with three balls inside, two black and one white or vice versa; the left side of the box is shaded with cross lines, the front with diagonal lines and the right side with vertical lines.

9 **a** The missing square is a vertical reflection of the last square on the bottom row.

10 **c** The line shapes in the central four squares are separated out one into each of the adjacent outer grid squares. The missing square contains the right-hand symbol from the square above it.

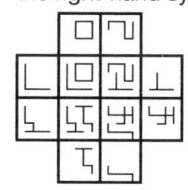

11 **e** The circle follows the pattern of –two white– one black– along both rows, the diagonal line pointing into the squares from a corner which rotates clockwise around the squares in the top row and anti-clockwise in the bottom row. The outside lines closest to the grid squares follow the repeating pattern of zigzag–plain– dashed, and the outer lines alternate between plain and dashed. The missing square must contain a black circle with a line to the bottom-

left corner; underneath the square will be a plain line with a dashed line beneath that.

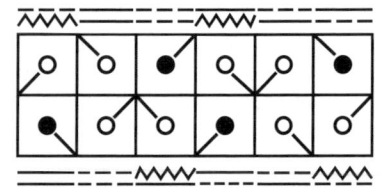

12 **e** The missing triangle will be a horizontal reflection of the triangle above it, with the white and grey shading swapped.

13 **c** The missing square will contain a large circle with diagonal cross-hatching and a small black triangle.

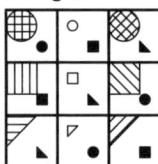

14 **b** The missing square will contain a small white square and a square with horizontal line shading in the bottom-right corner.

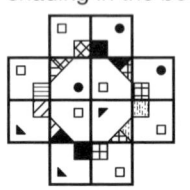

15 **e** The narrow rectangles in the top left corner follow the pattern three, two, one then back to three. The squares and circles in the top-right corner alternate; the shading within them follows the repeating sequence of –white–cross–black–. The orientation of the white triangle alternates while the black triangle is always in the same position. The curved arrow alternates between clockwise and anti-clockwise (its orientation is not relevant). So, the missing square will contain one narrow rectangle at the top left, a black circle at top right, a white triangle in the bottom-right corner with its vertical side in the middle and a clockwise arrow.

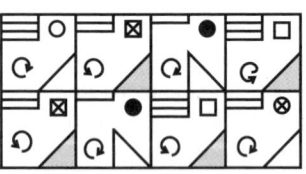

16 **c** The missing square will have the same shapes as the other squares in the first column, with the short line and the black spot below the second short line.

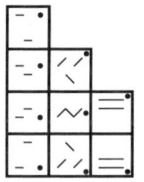

17 **a** The number of rows and columns in the second pattern is determined by the number of small shapes in the first circle. Each style of shading seen in the circles in the first pattern is represented in each row and each column of the grid.

18 **e** To form the second shape, the quadrilateral has become a circle, with the number of concentric rings determined by the number of 'bows' on the kite tail in the first shape; a small copy of the quadrilateral appears at the end of the tail in the second shape; the lines within the quadrilateral have become short lines across the tail.

19 **e** To form the second pattern, the crosses have become small black circles within a large circle and a number of other small shapes have been added so that the total number of small shapes in the second pattern matches the total number of sides of the two large shapes in the first pattern; one of the new small shapes is shaded with lines and the others are white.

20 **e** The second pattern is the first pattern broken up into sections; the straight sections have been arranged in a horizontal block and the curved/zigzag sections have been arranged in a vertical block.

21 **d** To form the second pattern, the small shapes along the 'thread' in the first pattern have become loops on a circular line; the two shapes at the end have been retained but black shapes have become white and vice versa; the number of black dots at the centre of the second pattern is determined by the number of small circles along the 'thread' in the first pattern.

22 **c** The second shape has the small symbols in the first shape repeated at the centre; each symbol from the first shape is also copied in the diagonally opposite corner of the second shape.

23 **d** The second shape is a 90° clockwise rotation of the first shape; the dashed lines have become plain lines; the plain arrowhead has changed to a white arrowhead; the black and white circles have exchanged shading.

24 **d** The second pattern is a 90° anticlockwise rotation of the first pattern; the lines have become thin rectangles and the dots have become small black circles.

25–32 When each shape is paired with the correct reflection, they form a single shape that is perfectly symmetrical.

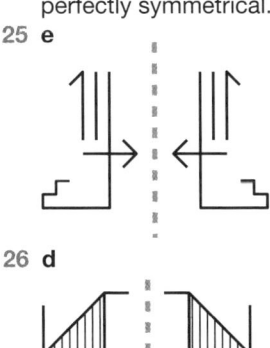

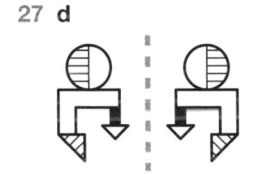

25 **e**

26 **d**

27 **d**

28 **e**

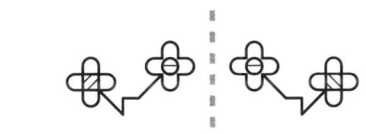

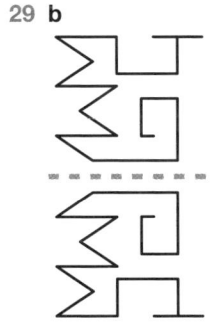

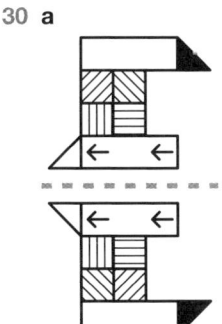

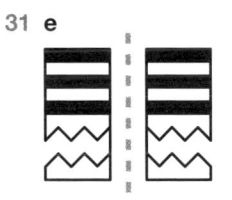

29 **b**

30 **a**

31 **e**

32 **c**

33 **c** The number of black spots decreases by one; the arrow rotates 90° anticlockwise and the L-shape rotates 90° clockwise; the shading of the square follows a repeating pattern of –diagonal (bottom left to top right)–diagonal (top left to bottom right)–cross-hatching–; the two short horizontal lines are constant.

34 **e** The style of the outline alternates between a solid and a dashed outer line; the number of pairs of black spots alternates between two and four; the number of single white circles increases by one each time.

35 **e** One more horizontal line becomes dashed each time, working from the bottom; the two small circles move up the shape from corner to corner, the white one following the black one; the circle with the cross alternates between the bottom and top space; the cross moves down the shape.

36 **c** The orientation of the Z at the top of the shape alternates and the tail on the Z-shape at the bottom follows a repeating pattern of –T-shape–pointing up–pointing down–; the first row of shapes has a small rectangle alternating with a circle or an oval; the second row follows a repeating pattern of –circle–shaded oval–white oval– .

37 **a** In alternate shapes a curved arrow threads up from behind into the top loop of the figure-of-eight-shape then out over the edge and then up again into the middle; these figure-of-eight shapes alternate with ones where the curved arrow threads down from the front into the top loop then up and around the outside and so on; in the lower loop of the figure-of-eight shape the number of black spots follows a repeating pattern of –one–two–three–; the number of lines in the zigzag shape decreases by one each time.

38 **e** The thin rectangles at the top decrease by one each time; the triangle moves down the right side of the square; the dashes at the bottom decrease by one each time; the orientation of the double L-shapes alternates.

39 **c** The lines of the main shape become dashed one by one, working alternately from the bottom and the top; the style of the separate vertical and horizontal lines alternates between solid and dashed.

40 **d** The shapes follow a repeating pattern of –circle–triangle–square–; this applies to both the outer shapes and the inner shapes, so the next shape will be a triangle with a circle inside and a square overlapping one of its sides; the shading of the square follows a repeating pattern of –horizontal lines–black shading–diagonal lines– (except where the square overlaps another shape, or is partly outside the outer shape, where that section is white); The style of the line underneath the outer shape alternates between solid and dashed.

41 **e** When the right-angled triangle is on the front of the cube and the U-shape is on the left, the L-shape will be on the top but it will have its corner at the far left, not the far right.

42 **d** The striped triangle on the face divided into quarters, not the black triangle, is adjacent to the inverted U-shape.

43 **b** When the double arrow is on the front of the cube and the face with the black bar is on the right, one of the right-angled triangles will be on the top, but it will have its right angle at the far right, not the far left.

44 **e** When the black semi-circle is on the top of the cube and the face with the two bars is on the left, the U-shape is on the front but it is not inverted.

45 **e** When the V-shape is on the front of the cube, orientated as shown, the circle will be on the left but the diagonal lines within it will go from top left to bottom right, not bottom left to top right.

46 **b** When the U-shape with the spot is on the front of the cube and the arrow is on the left, the half-black face will be on the top, but the black half will be at the front, not the back.

47 **c** The four parallel lines and the arrow are in opposite positions, therefore they cannot be seen as adjacent faces on the cube.

48 **d** When the N-shape is on the front of the cube, the triangle will be on the top or the bottom, not one of the sides.

49 **c** The first letter represents the length of the lines that form the L-shape (A has lines of equal length and B has one line longer than the other). The second letter represents the position and colour of the small square at the corner (P has a small white square outside the corner, Q has a small white square inside the corner, R has a small black square outside the corner and S has a small black square inside the corner). The third letter represents the number of short lines crossing the L-shape (L has one, M has two and N has three).

50 **d** The first letter represents the number of sides the main shape has (A has five sides, B has six and C has eight). The second letter represents the shading of the smaller shape (R has diagonal lines, Q has horizontal lines and S has vertical/horizontal cross-hatching, so by deduction T has vertical lines). The third letter represents the number of short lines crossing the outline (L has one, M has two, N has three and O has four).

51 **c** The first letter represents the shading of the small rectangle (A has solid white shading, B has diagonal lines, C has vertical lines and D has solid black shading). The second letter represents the style of the short line crossing the outline of the triangle (X has a straight line, Y has a curled line and Z has an arrow). The third letter represents the side of the triangle where the short line crosses (E has the line crossing the vertical side, F has the line crossing the horizontal side and G has the line crossing the hypotenuse).

52 **e** The first letter represents the linkage of the large shapes (A has all the shapes inside one of the shapes, B has one shape inside another with one overlapping and C has the three shapes linked in a chain). The second letter represents the number and shading of any overlapping sections (J has one black section, L has two black sections and M has two lined sections, so by deduction K has one lined section). The third letter represents the shape in which the black spot is located (X has the black spot in the circle, Y has it in the triangle and Z has it in the square).

53 **b** The first letter represents the position of the wider circle or cylinder (L has the wider circle or cylinder at the bottom of the shape, M has it on the left and N has it at the top). The second letter represents the pattern in the shaded rings around the cylinder (A has a black and zigzag pattern, B has a plain black ring, C has a zigzag pattern and D has no pattern). The third letter represents the shading of the end circular face (X has lines, Y has solid black shading and Z has solid white circle).

54 **d** The first letter represents the number of lines projecting at the bottom left of the shape (A has three lines, B has two and C has one). The second letter represents the number of lines projecting at Wthe bottom right of the shape

(E has two lines, F has one and G has four). The third letter represents the number of lines projecting at the top right (S has two lines, T has three and U has four).

55 **e** The first letter represents the pattern and orientation of the thin rectangle (A has a vertical rectangle with zigzag lines, B has a vertical rectangle with horizontal lines and C has a horizontal rectangle with zigzag lines, so by deduction D has a horizontal rectangle with vertical lines). The second letter represents the number of lines in the zigzag section (P has three lines, Q has four and R has five, so by deduction S has six). The third letter represents the number of loops in the coil along the top (N has one and M has two).

56 **b** The first letter represents the line shading style behind the circle on the front face of the cube (A is diagonal lines from bottom left to top right, B has horizontal lines, C has diagonal lines from top left to bottom right and D has no shading). The second letter represents the number of circles seen (X has one circle, Y has two and Z has three). The third letter represents the orientation of the cube (J has its front face lower left, K has its front face lower right and L has its front face upper left, so by deduction M has its front face upper right).

57 **d** The second shape has been rotated 90° anticlockwise.

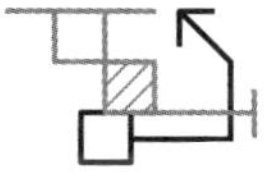

58 **c** The second shape has been rotated 90° anticlockwise.

59 **b** The first shape has been rotated 90° clockwise.

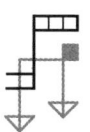

60 **c** The first shape has been rotated 90° anticlockwise. The second shape has been rotated 90° clockwise.

61 **d** The second shape has been rotated 180°.

62 **d** The first shape has been rotated 180°. The second shape has been rotated 90° anticlockwise.

63 **d** Neither shape has been rotated, they are overlapping. Shape consists of two and a half unequal 'steps'.

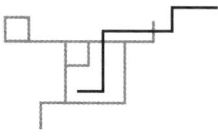

64 **a** Neither shape has been rotated, they are overlapping.

NOTES

Which shape or pattern completes the pattern on the left? Circle the letter.

Example

a b **(c)** d e

9

a b c d e

10

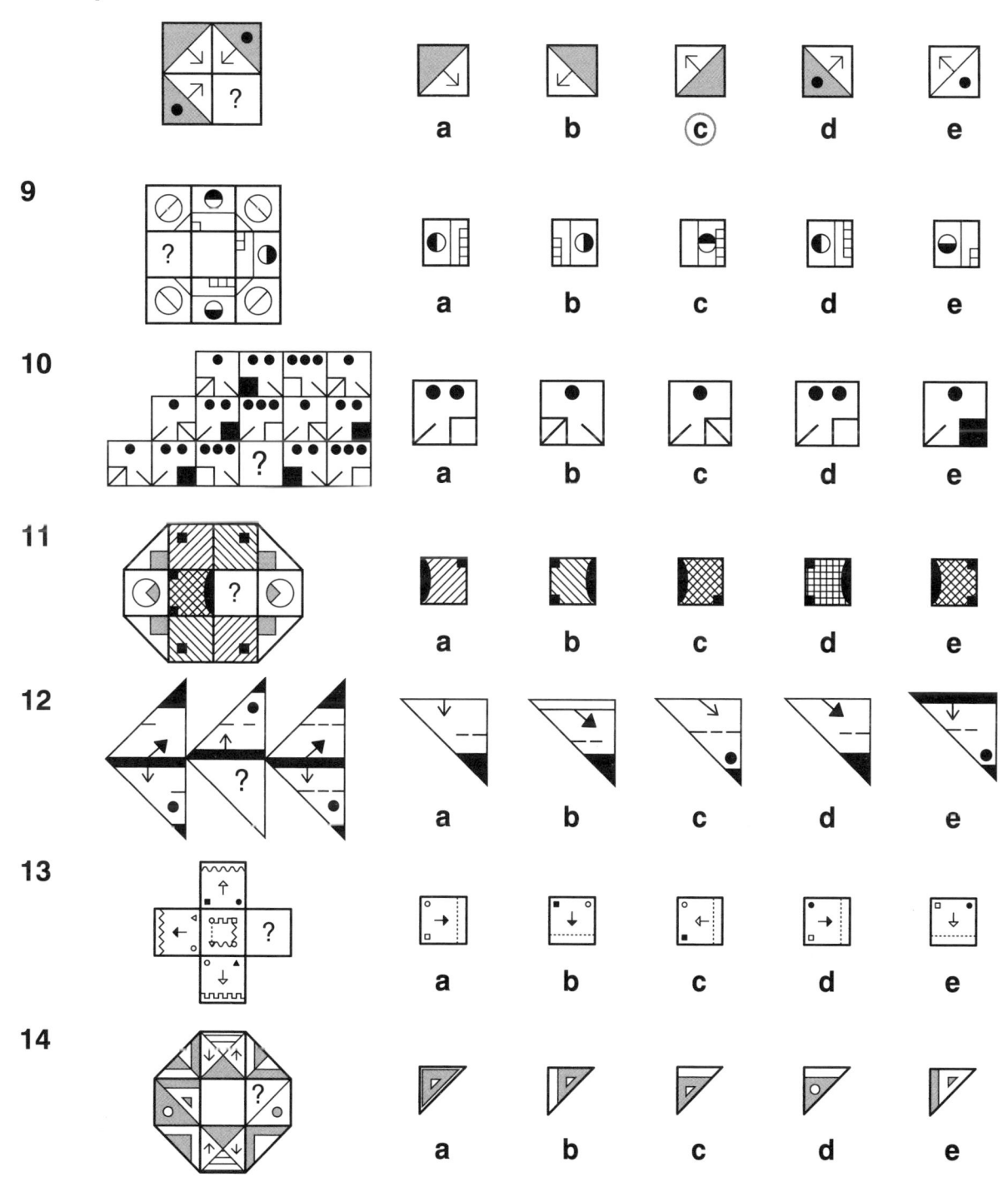

a b c d e

11

a b c d e

12

a b c d e

13

a b c d e

14

a b c d e

15

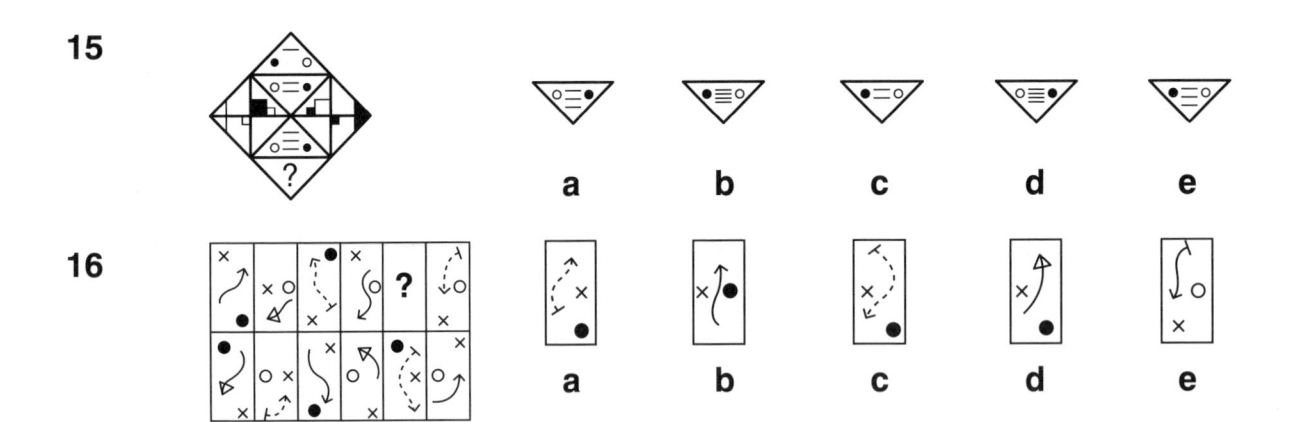

16

Which shape or pattern completes the second pair in the same way as the first pair? Circle the letter.

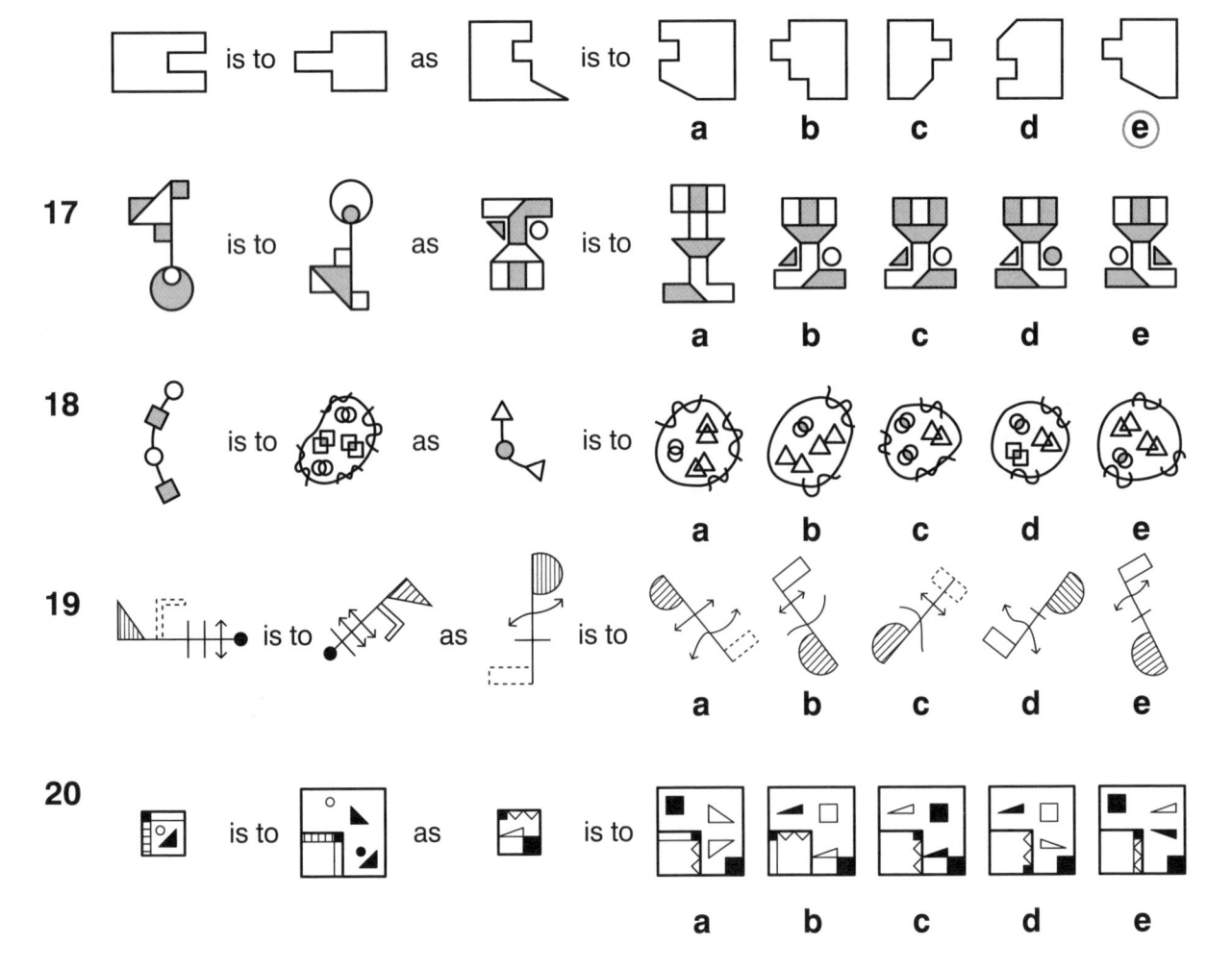

Example

is to ... as ... is to ... a b c d **(e)**

17 is to as is to a b c d e

18 is to as is to a b c d e

19 is to as is to a b c d e

20 is to as is to a b c d e

21 ... is to ... as ... is to ... a b c d e

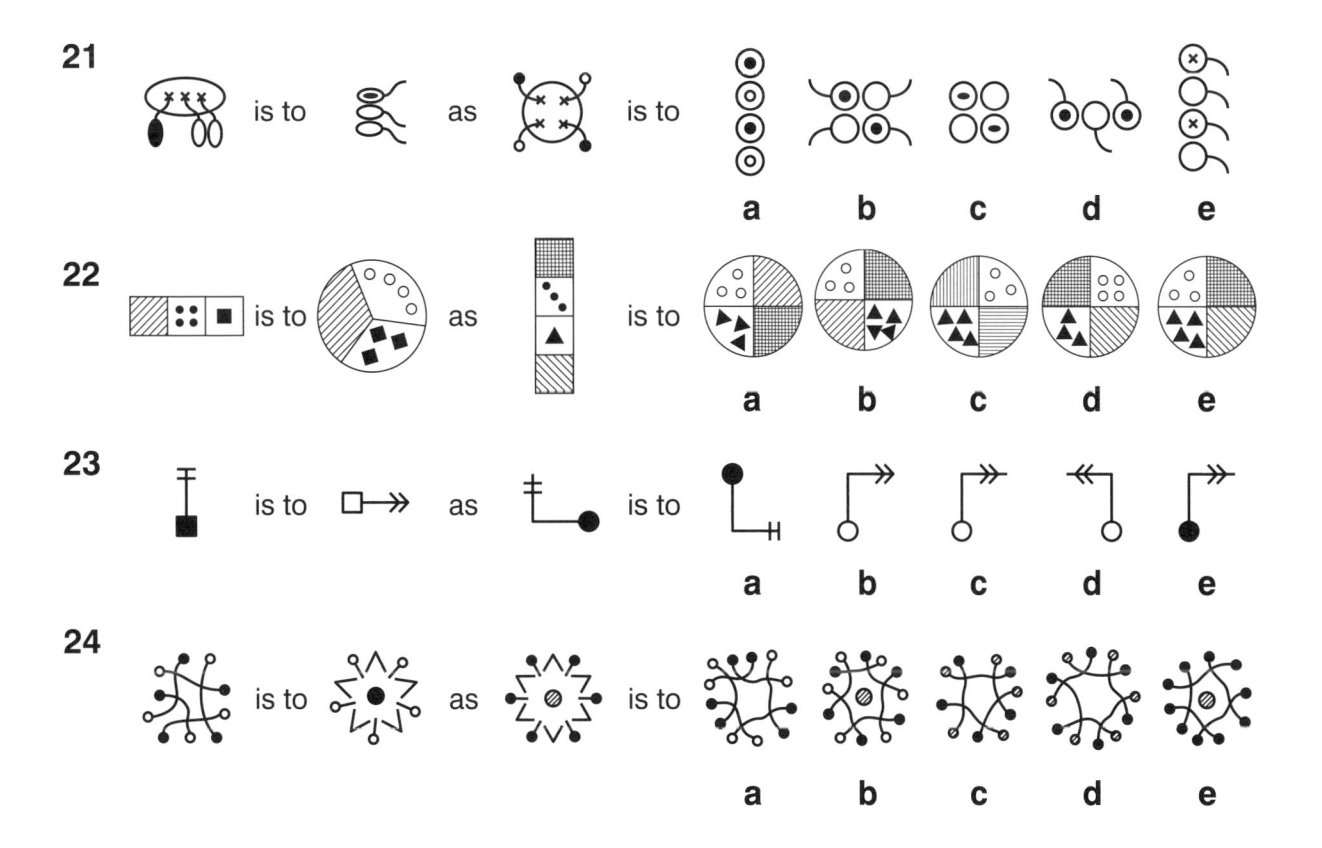

22 ... is to ... as ... is to ... a b c d e

23 ... is to ... as ... is to ... a b c d e

24 ... is to ... as ... is to ... a b c d e

Which shape or pattern is a reflection of the shape on the left? Circle the letter.

Example

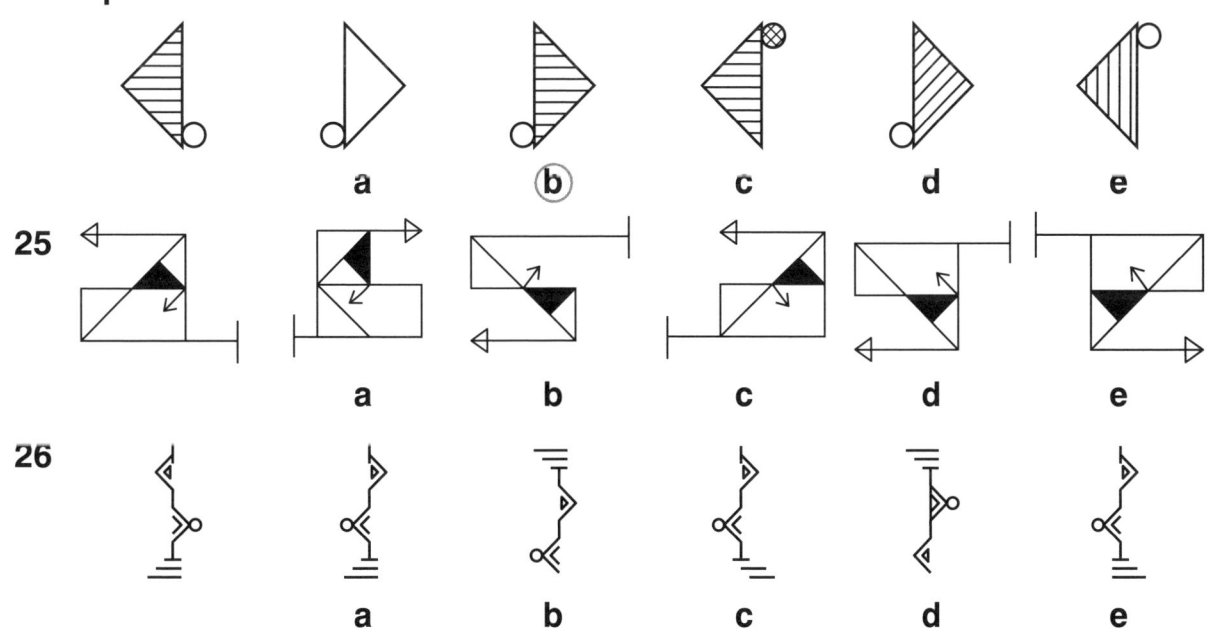

a (b) c d e

25 a b c d e

26 a b c d e

27 – **32**

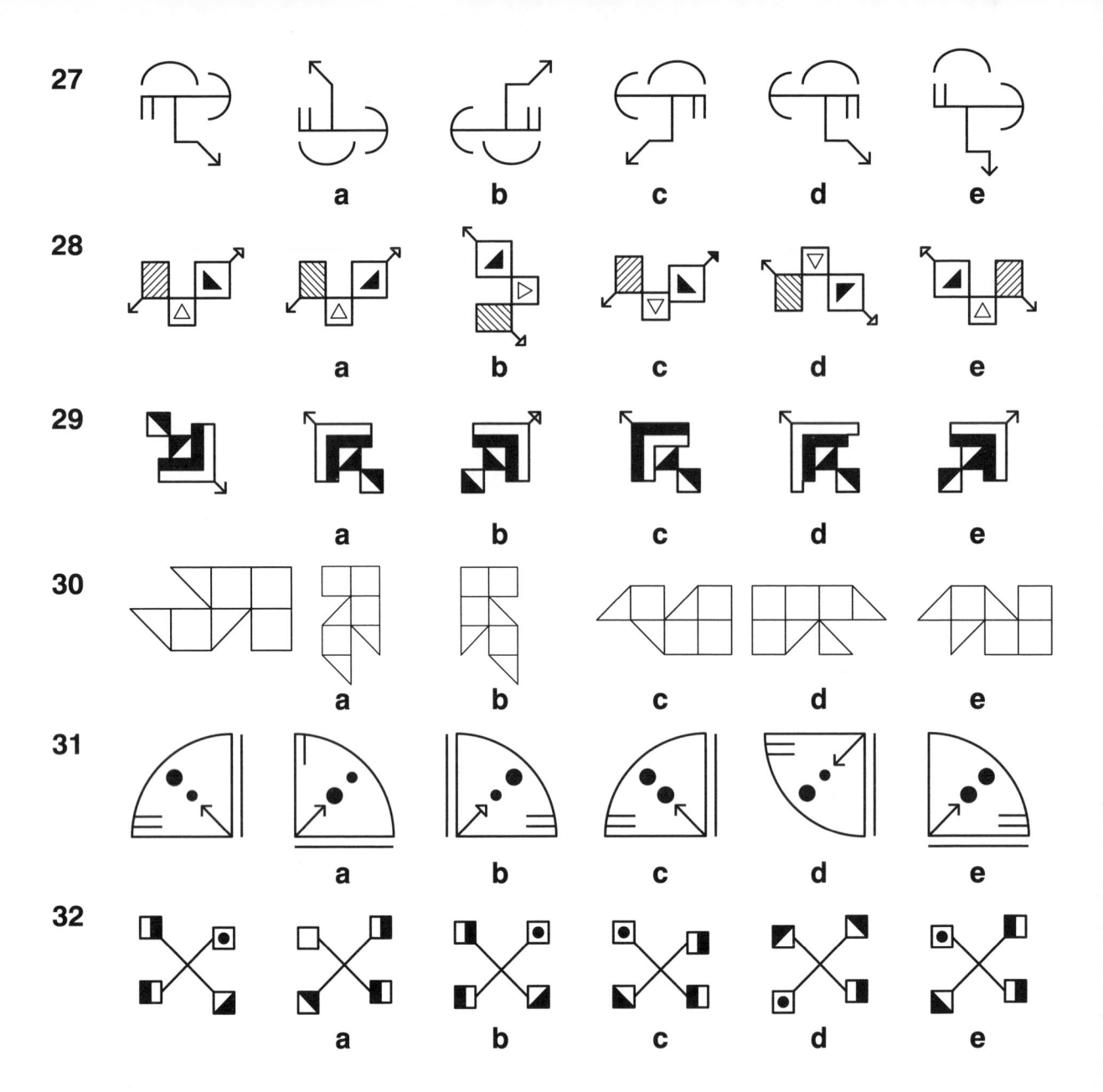

Which shape or pattern continues or completes the given sequence?
Circle the letter.

Example

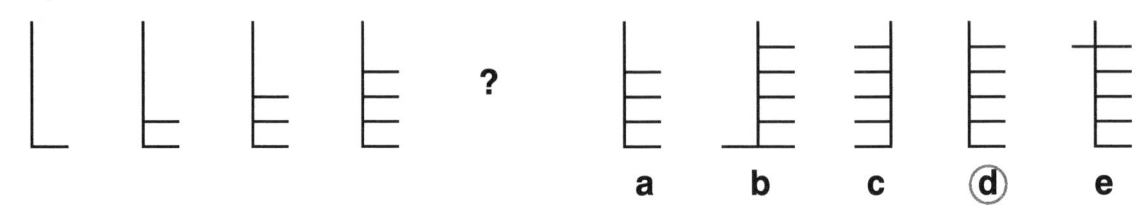

33 **34** **35** **36** **37** **38** **39** **40**

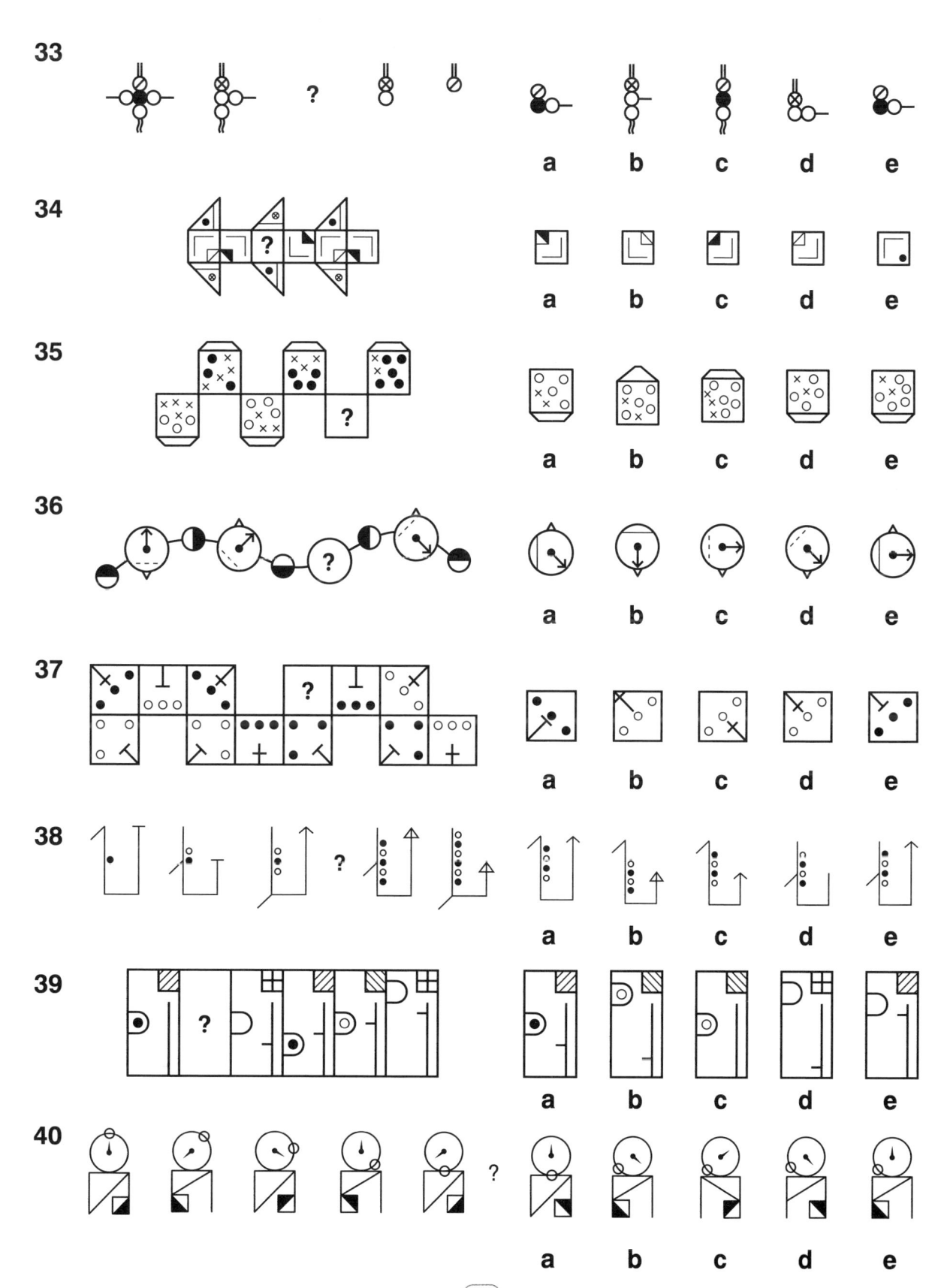

a b c d e

Which cube could not be made from the given net? Circle the letter.

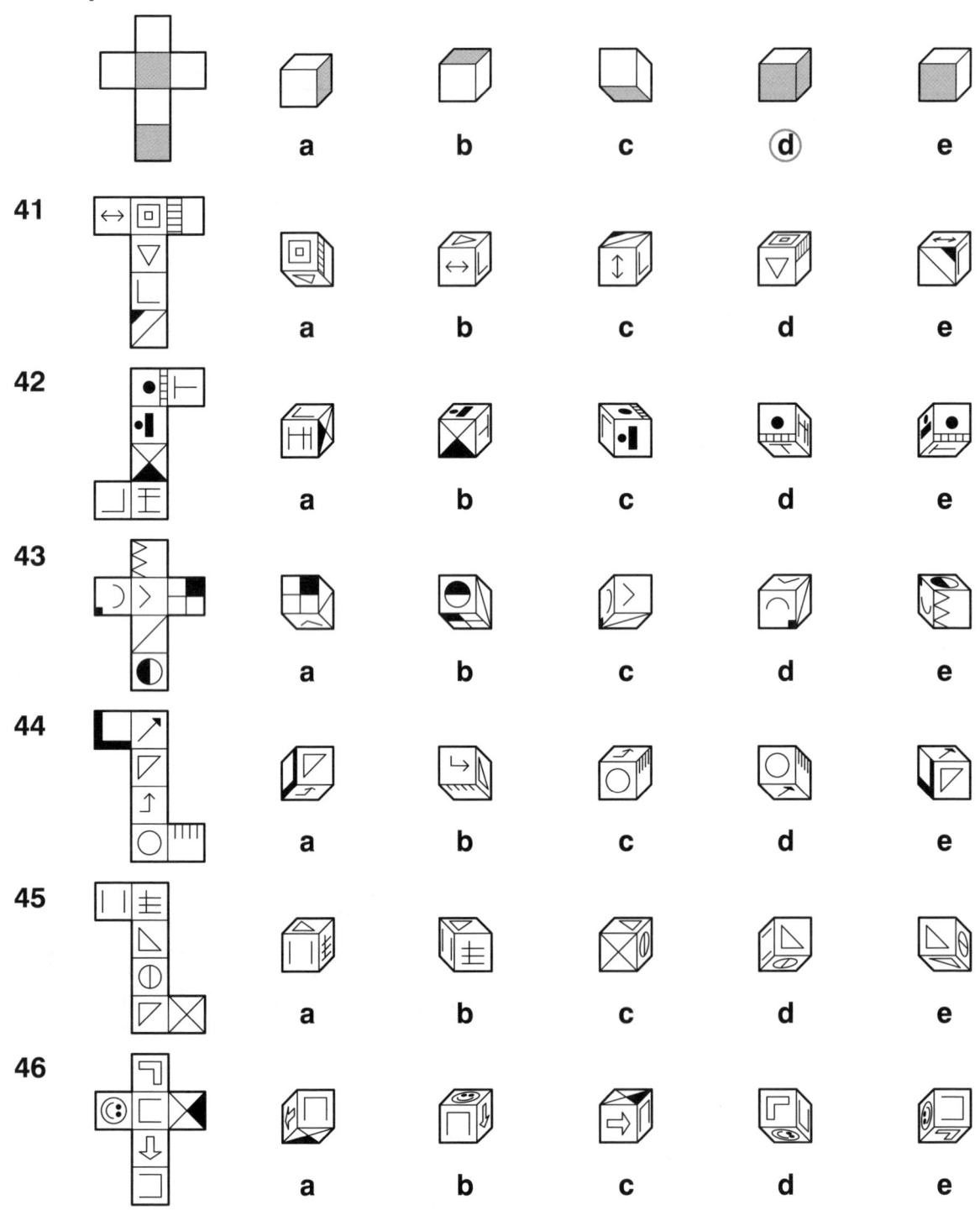

Example

a b c (d) e

41

a b c d e

42

a b c d e

43

a b c d e

44

a b c d e

45

a b c d e

46

a b c d e

47

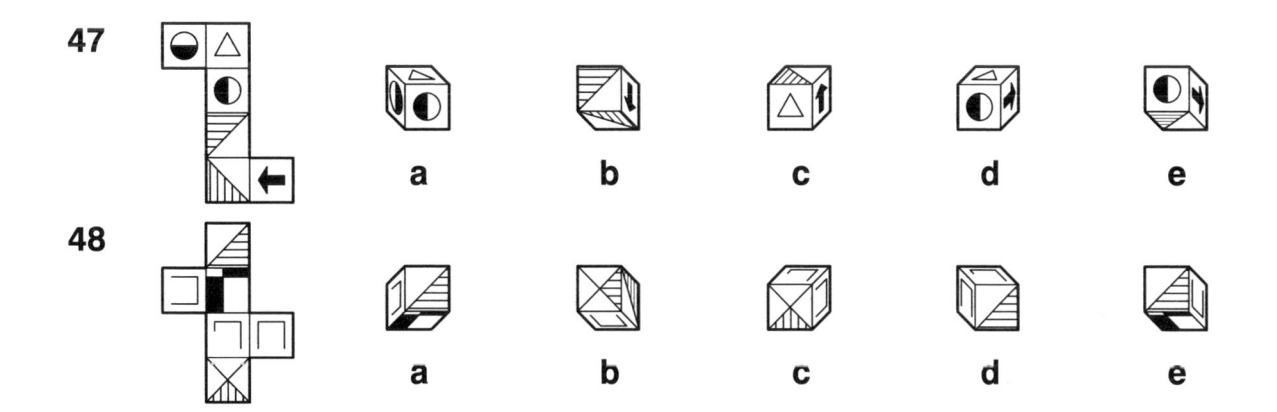

48

Using the given patterns and codes, work out the code that matches the last pattern. Circle the letter.

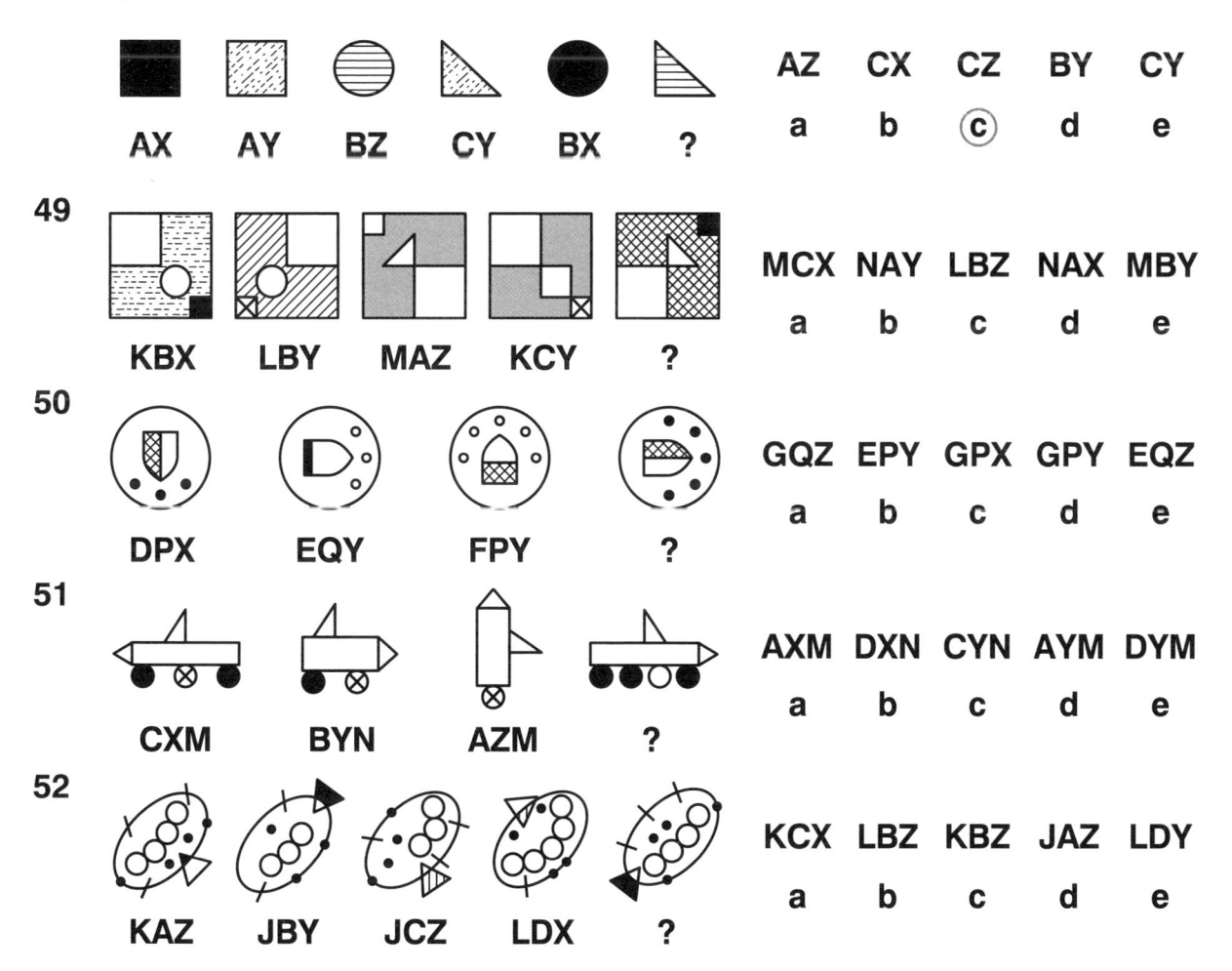

Example

AX AY BZ CY BX ?

AZ CX CZ BY CY
a   b   ⓒ   d   e

49

KBX LBY MAZ KCY ?

MCX NAY LBZ NAX MBY
a   b   c   d   e

50

DPX EQY FPY ?

GQZ EPY GPX GPY EQZ
a   b   c   d   e

51

CXM BYN AZM ?

AXM DXN CYN AYM DYM
a   b   c   d   e

52

KAZ JBY JCZ LDX ?

KCX LBZ KBZ JAZ LDY
a   b   c   d   e

53. LAT MCR NCT ?   MAR NBR NAS LBS MBS
                          a   b   c   d   e

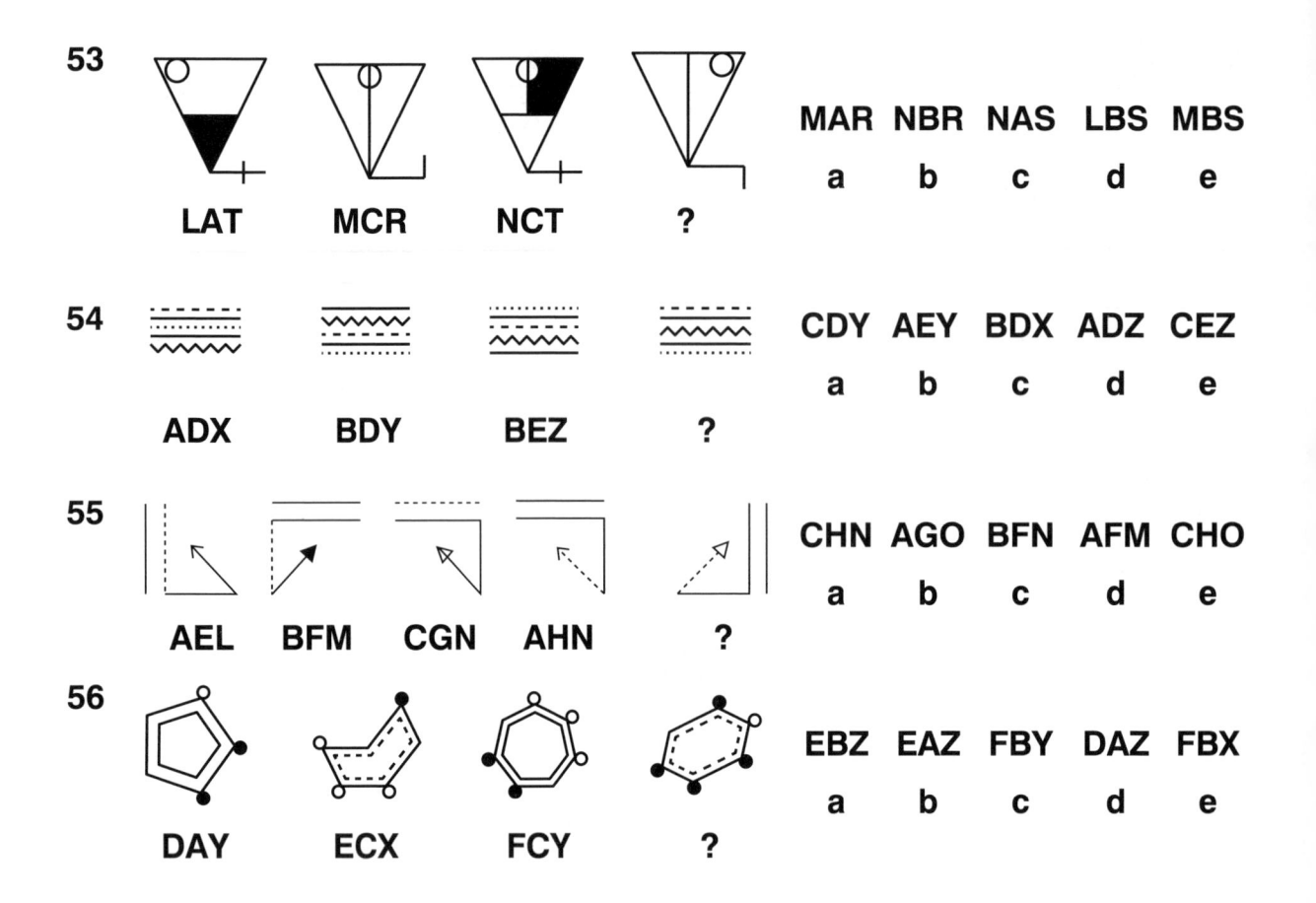

54. ADX BDY BEZ ?   CDY AEY BDX ADZ CEZ
                          a   b   c   d   e

55. AEL BFM CGN AHN ?   CHN AGO BFN AFM CHO
                          a   b   c   d   e

56. DAY ECX FCY ?   EBZ EAZ FBY DAZ FBX
                          a   b   c   d   e

Which pattern on the right is made by combining the two shapes on the left? Circle the letter.

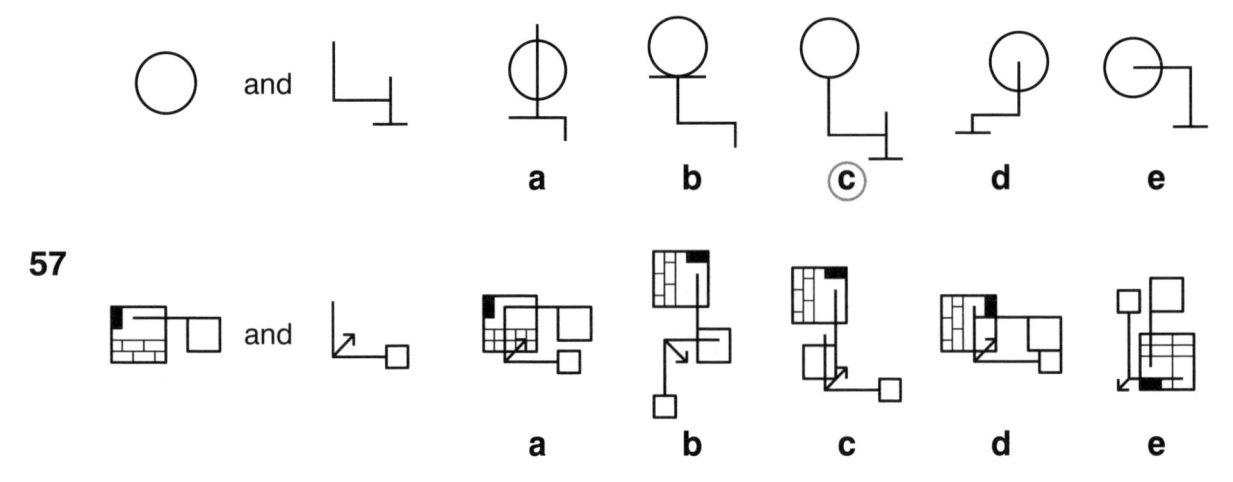

Example

57.

58

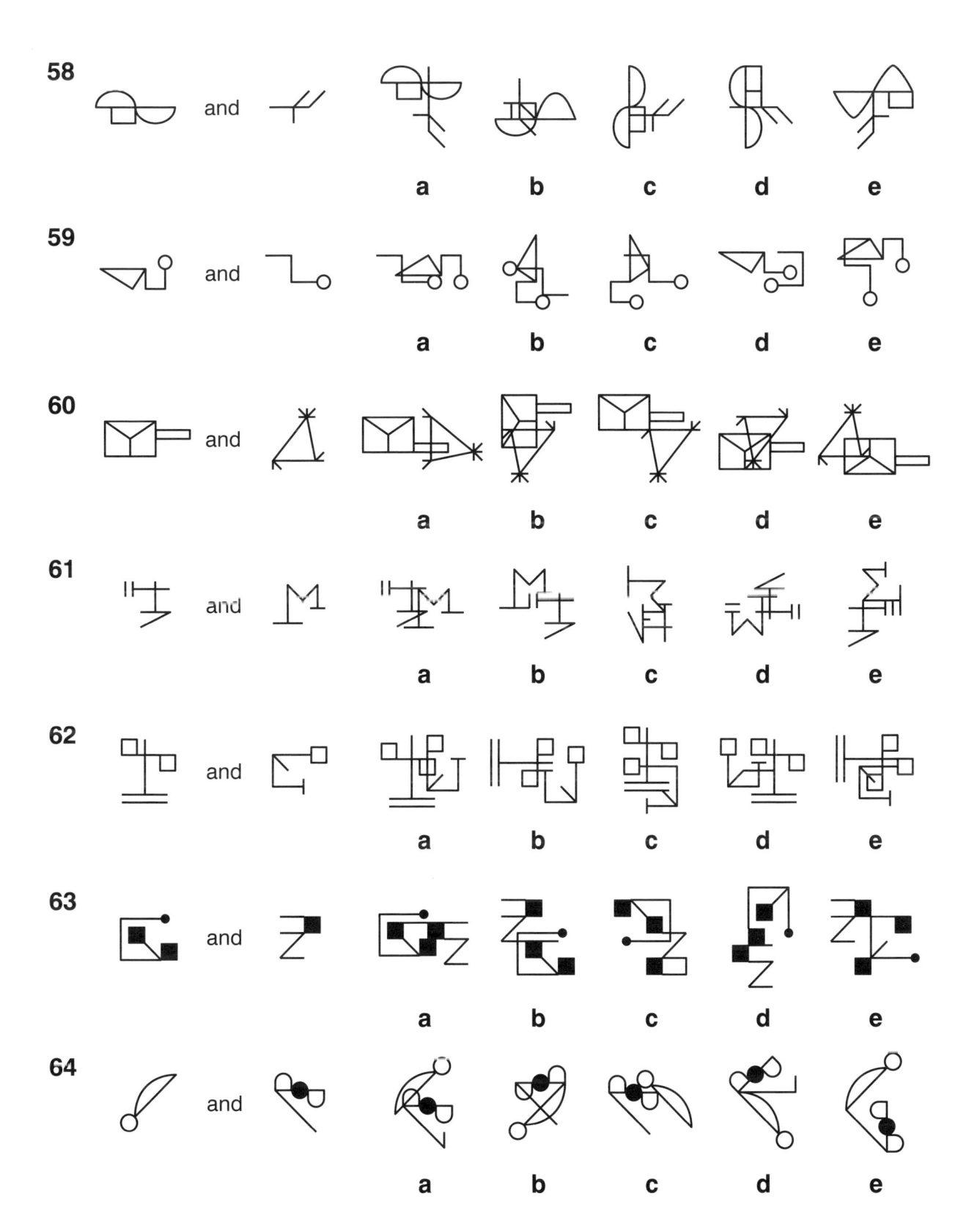

Mixed paper 3

Which of the shapes belongs to the group on the left? Circle the letter.

Example

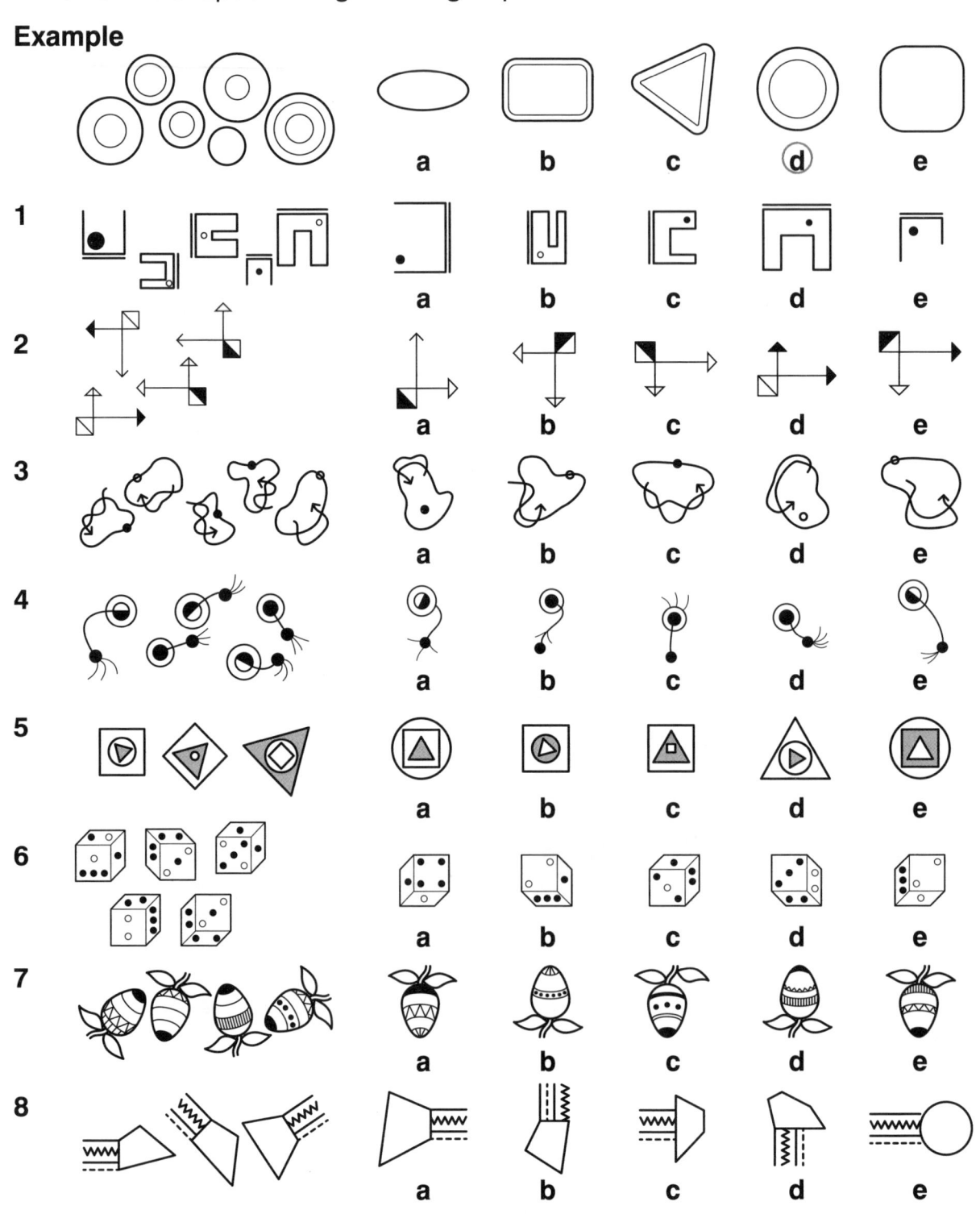

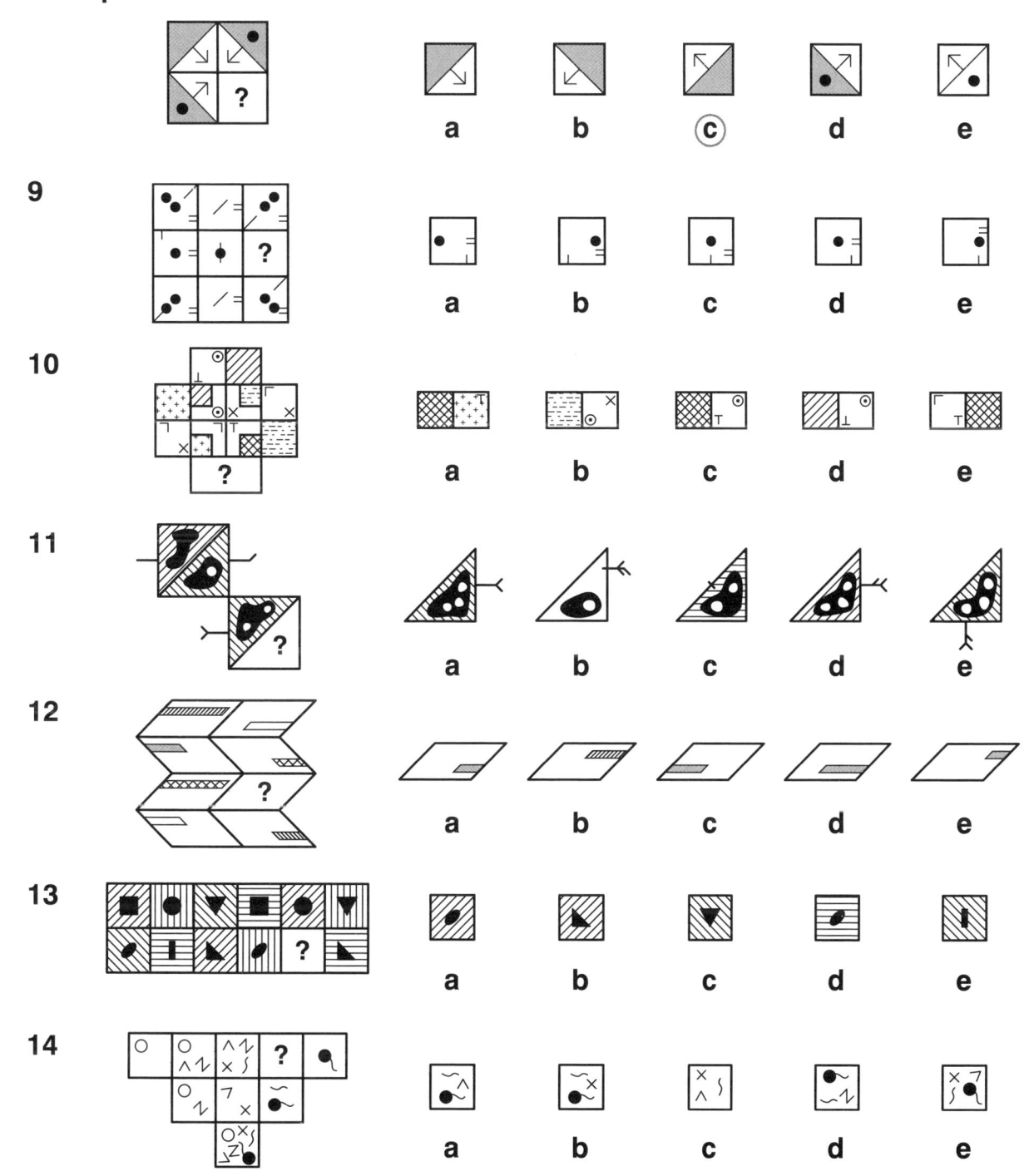

Which shape or pattern completes the pattern on the left? Circle the letter.

Example

a   b   ⓒ   d   e

9

a   b   c   d   e

10

a   b   c   d   e

11

a   b   c   d   e

12

a   b   c   d   e

13

a   b   c   d   e

14

a   b   c   d   e

15

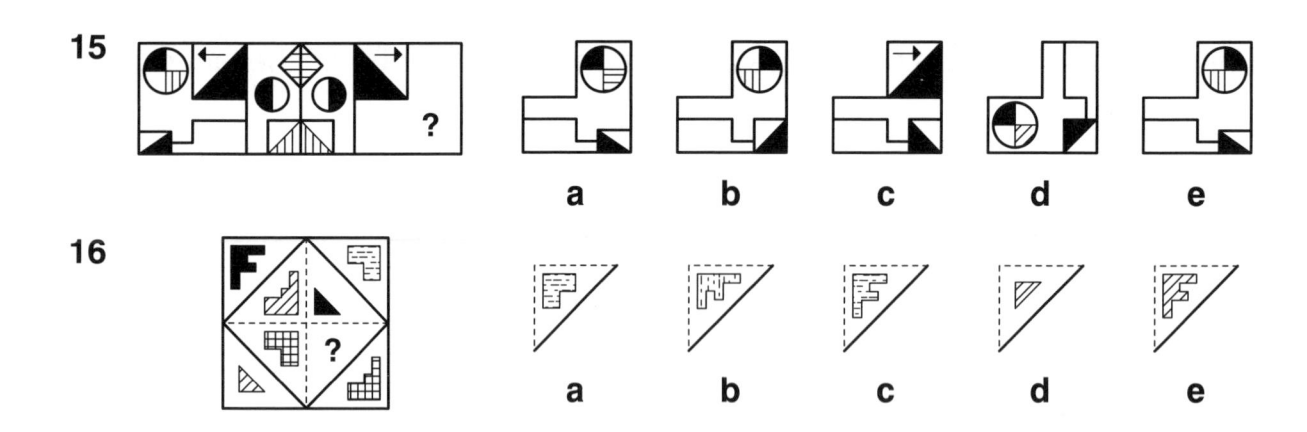

16

Which shape or pattern completes the second pair in the same way as the first pair? Circle the letter.

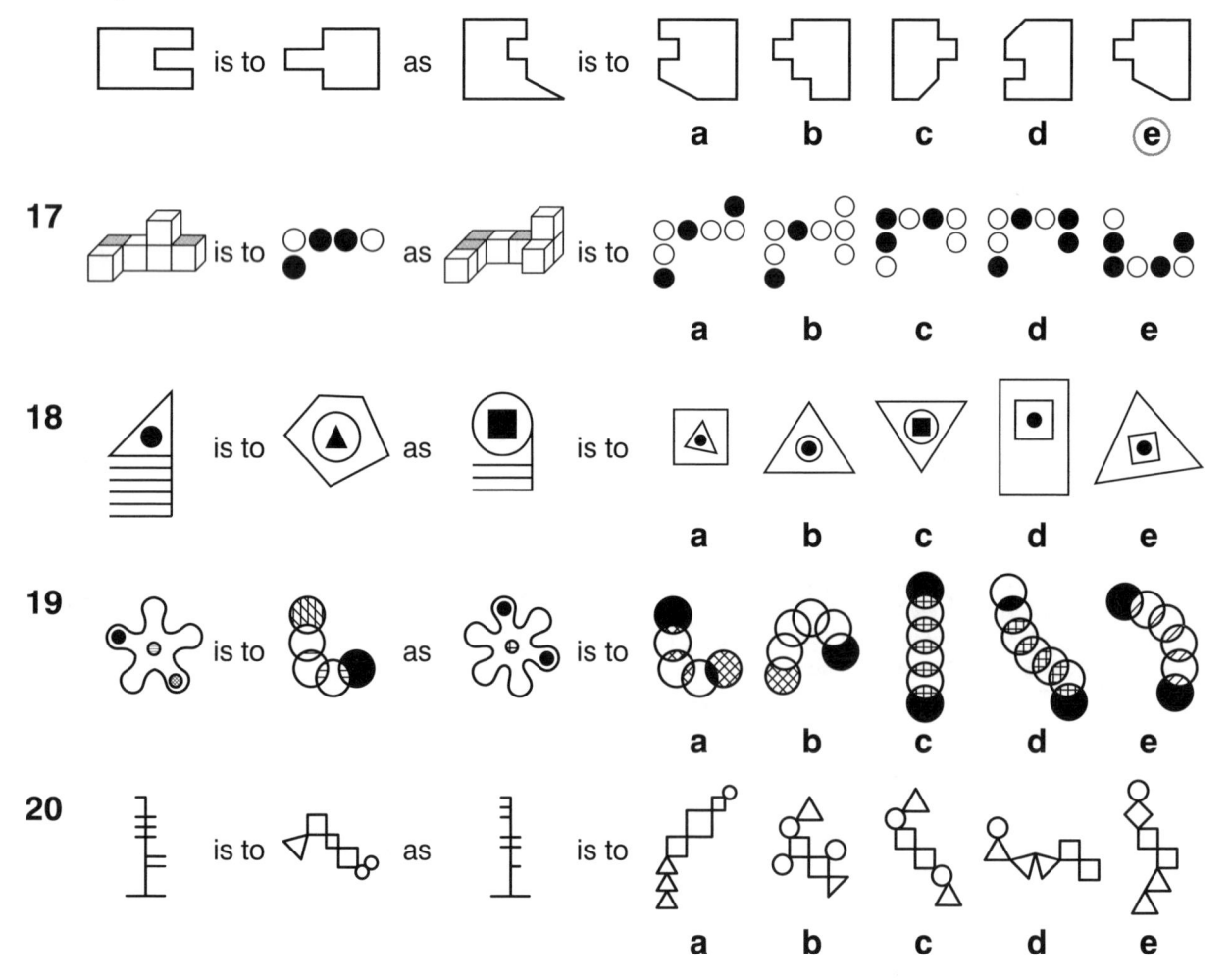

Example

is to ... as ... is to

a b c d e

17 is to ... as ... is to

a b c d e

18 is to ... as ... is to

a b c d e

19 is to ... as ... is to

a b c d e

20 is to ... as ... is to

a b c d e

21 ... is to ... as ... is to ... a b c d e

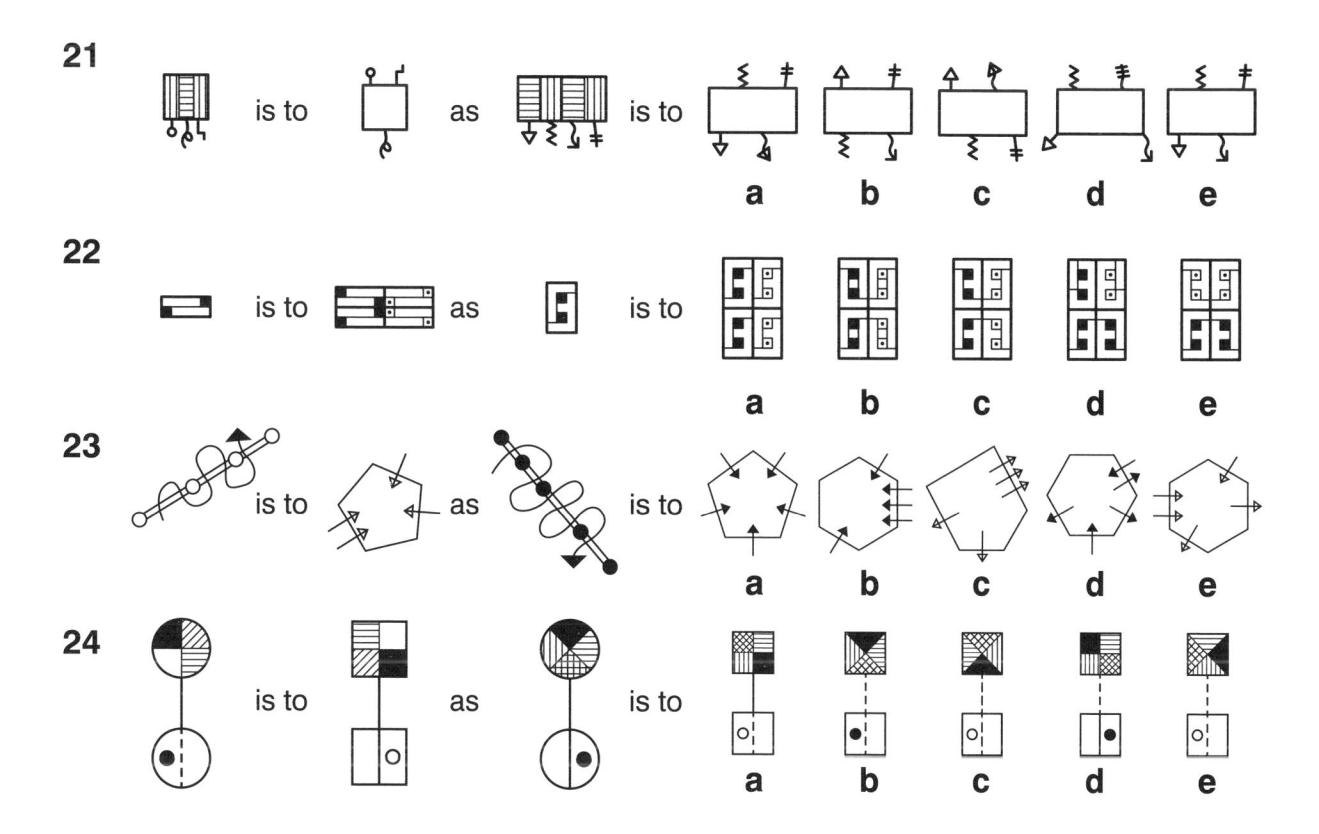

22 ... is to ... as ... is to ... a b c d e

23 ... is to ... as ... is to ... a b c d e

24 ... is to ... as ... is to ... a b c d e

Which shape or pattern is a reflection of the shape on the left? Circle the letter.

Example

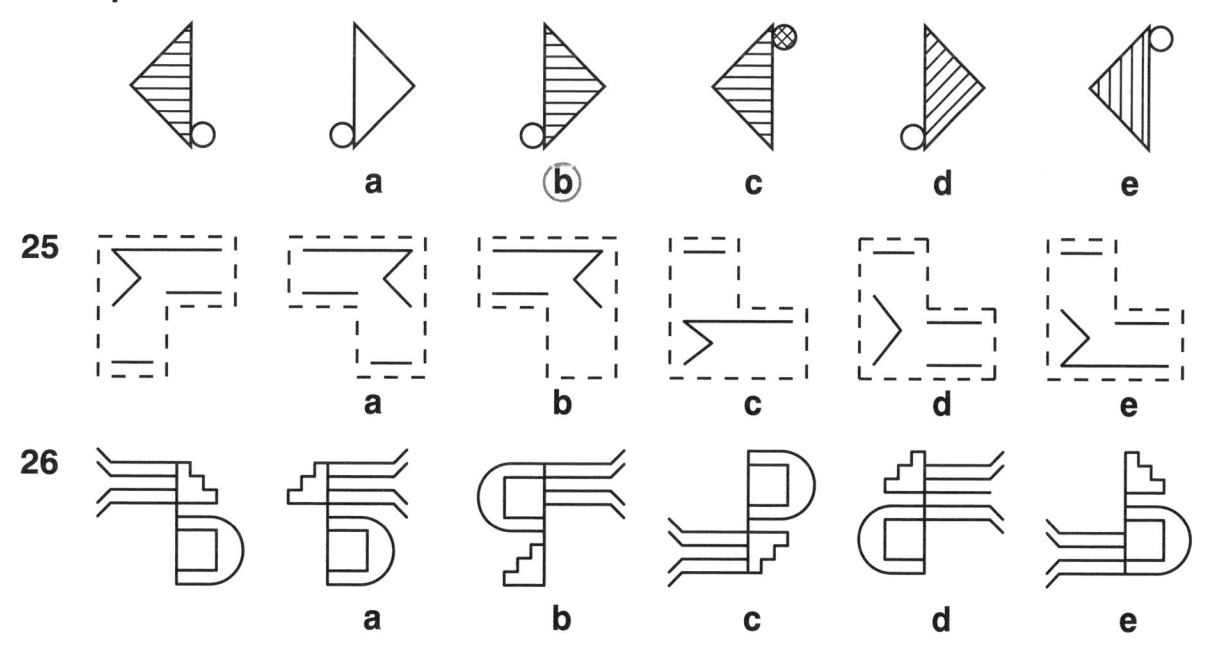

a (b) c d e

25 a b c d e

26 a b c d e

27

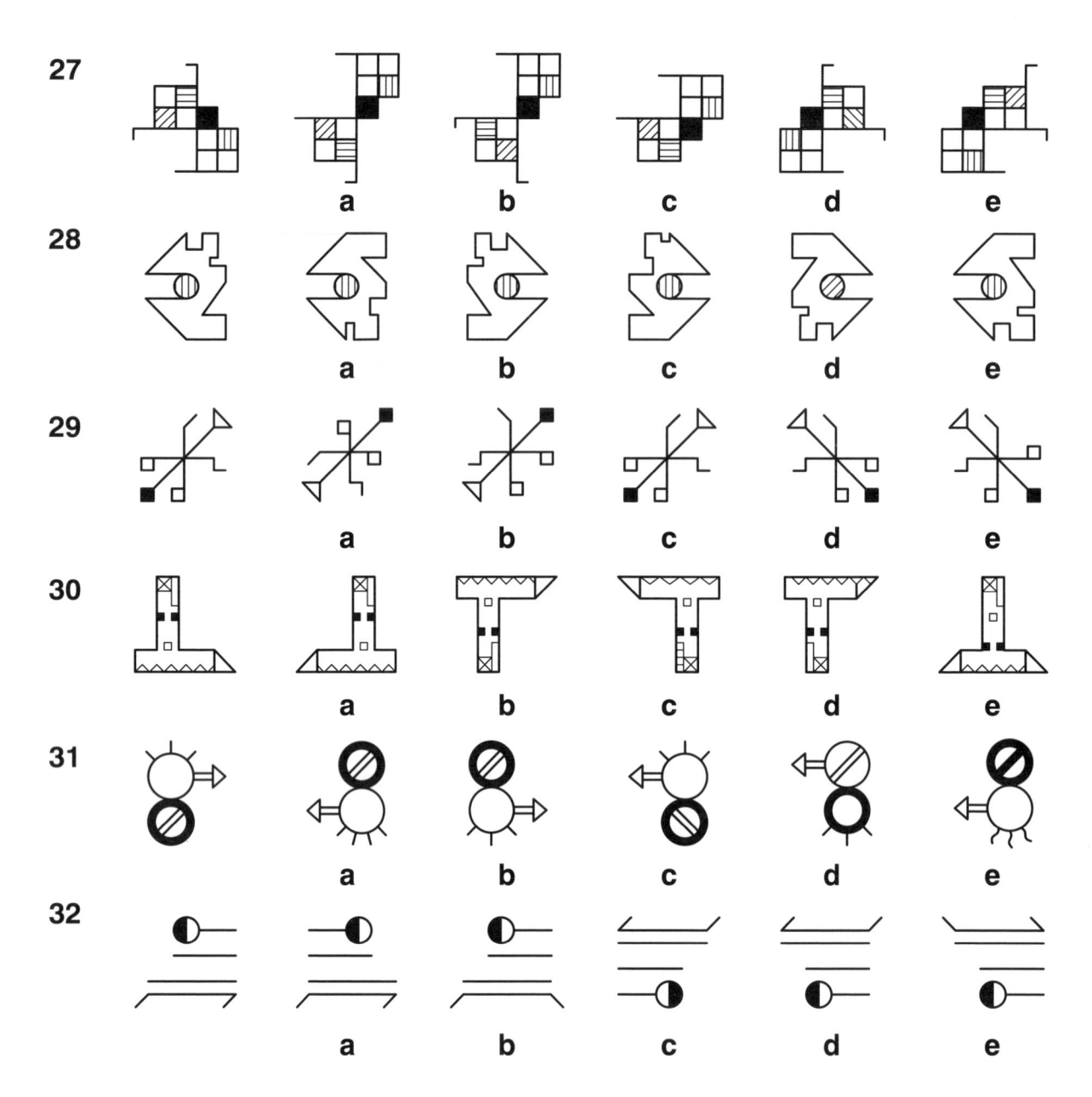

28

29

30

31

32

Which shape or pattern continues or completes the given sequence? Circle the letter.

Example

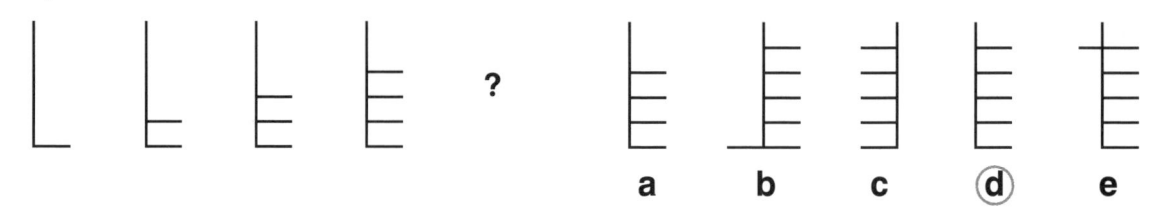

33

a b c d e

34

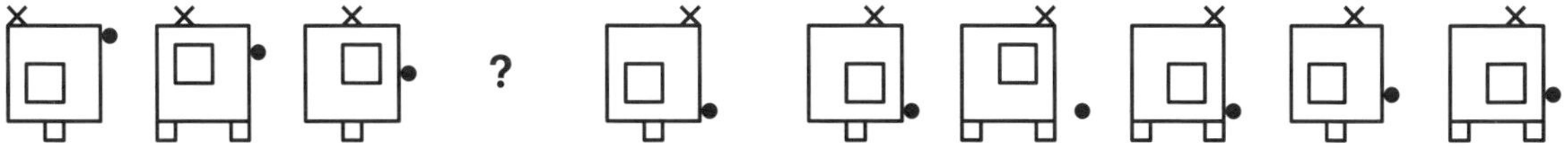

a b c d e

35

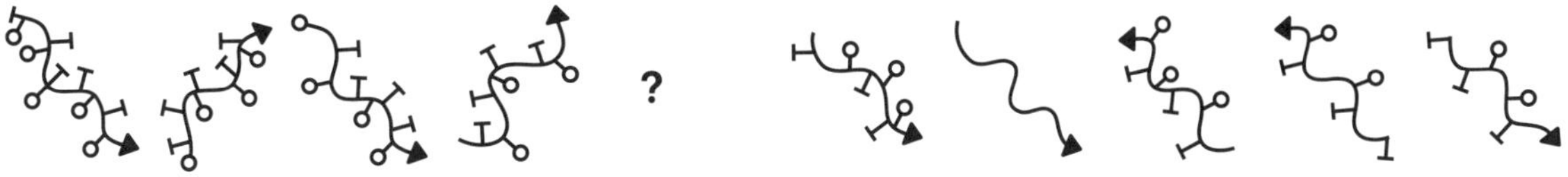

a b c d e

36

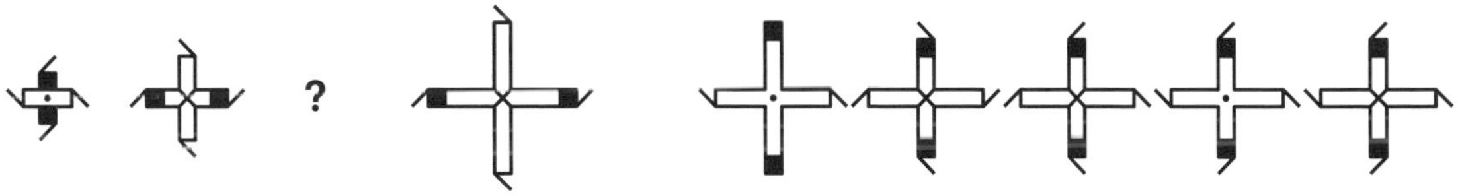

a b c d e

37

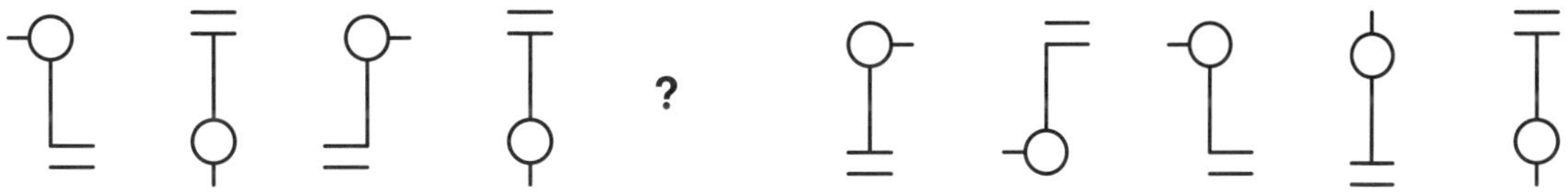

a b c d e

38

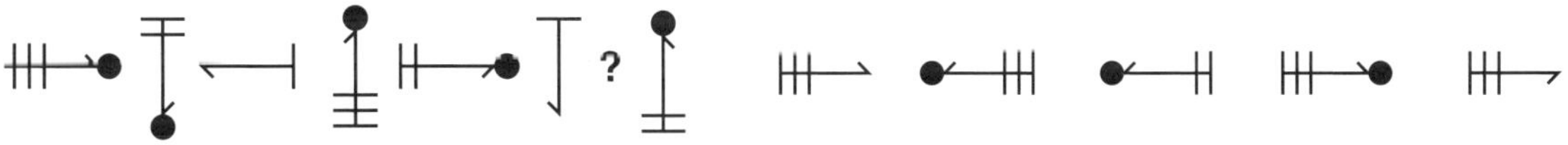

a b c d e

39

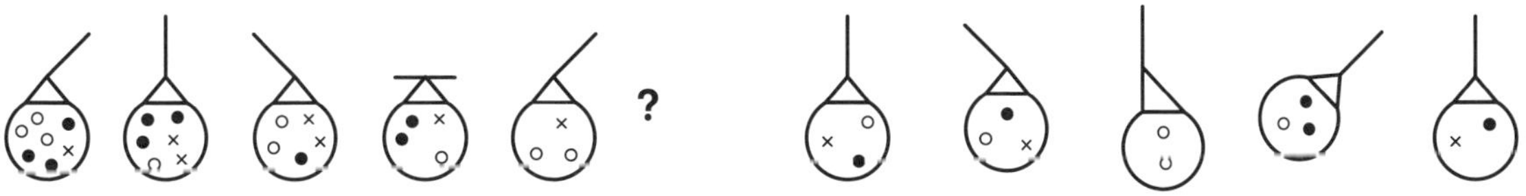

a b c d e

40

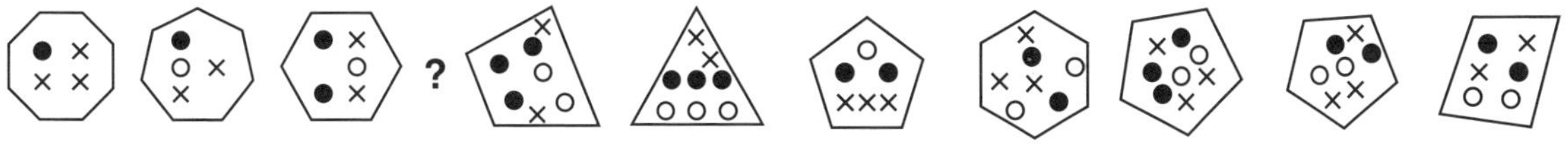

a b c d e

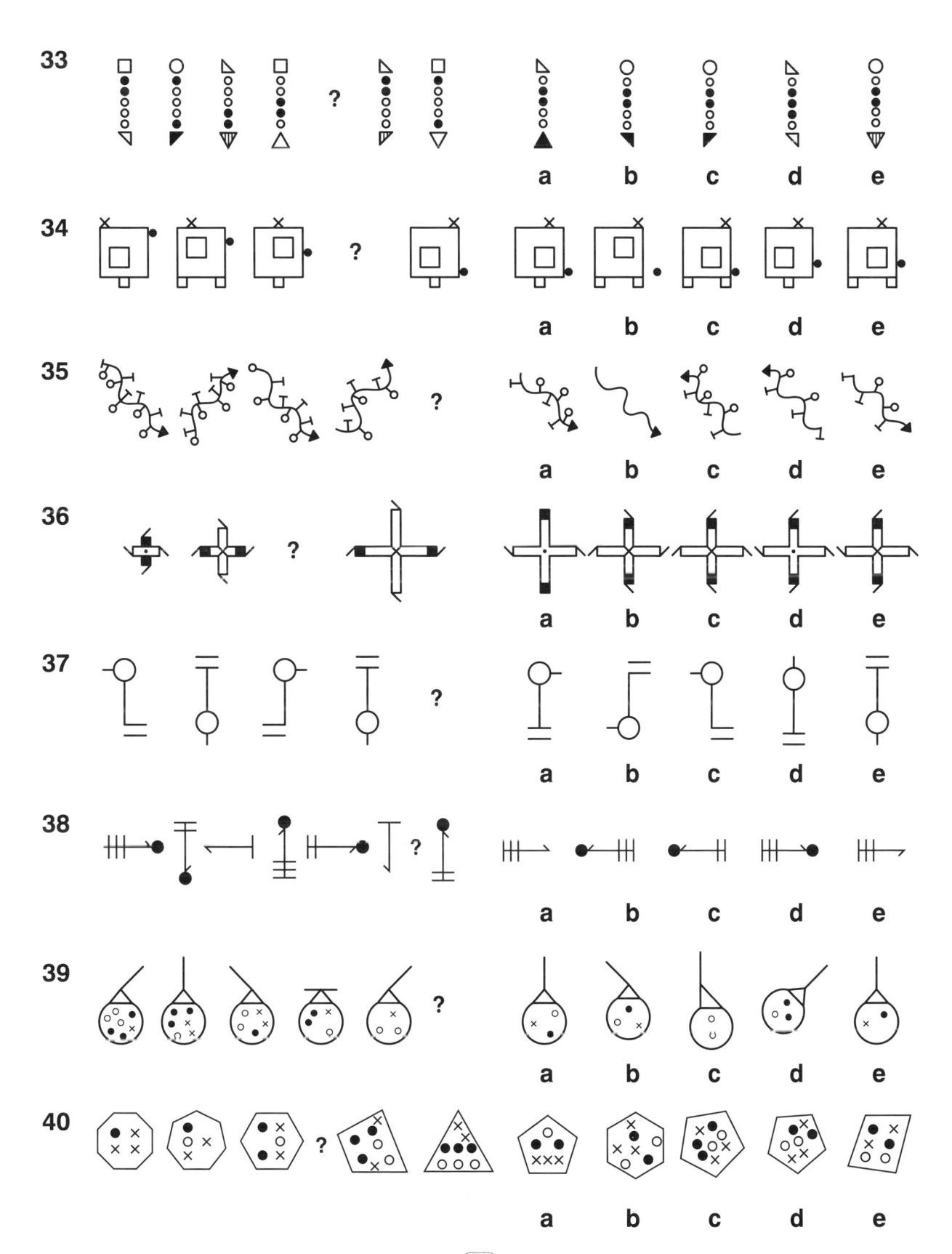

Which cube could not be made from the given net? Circle the letter.

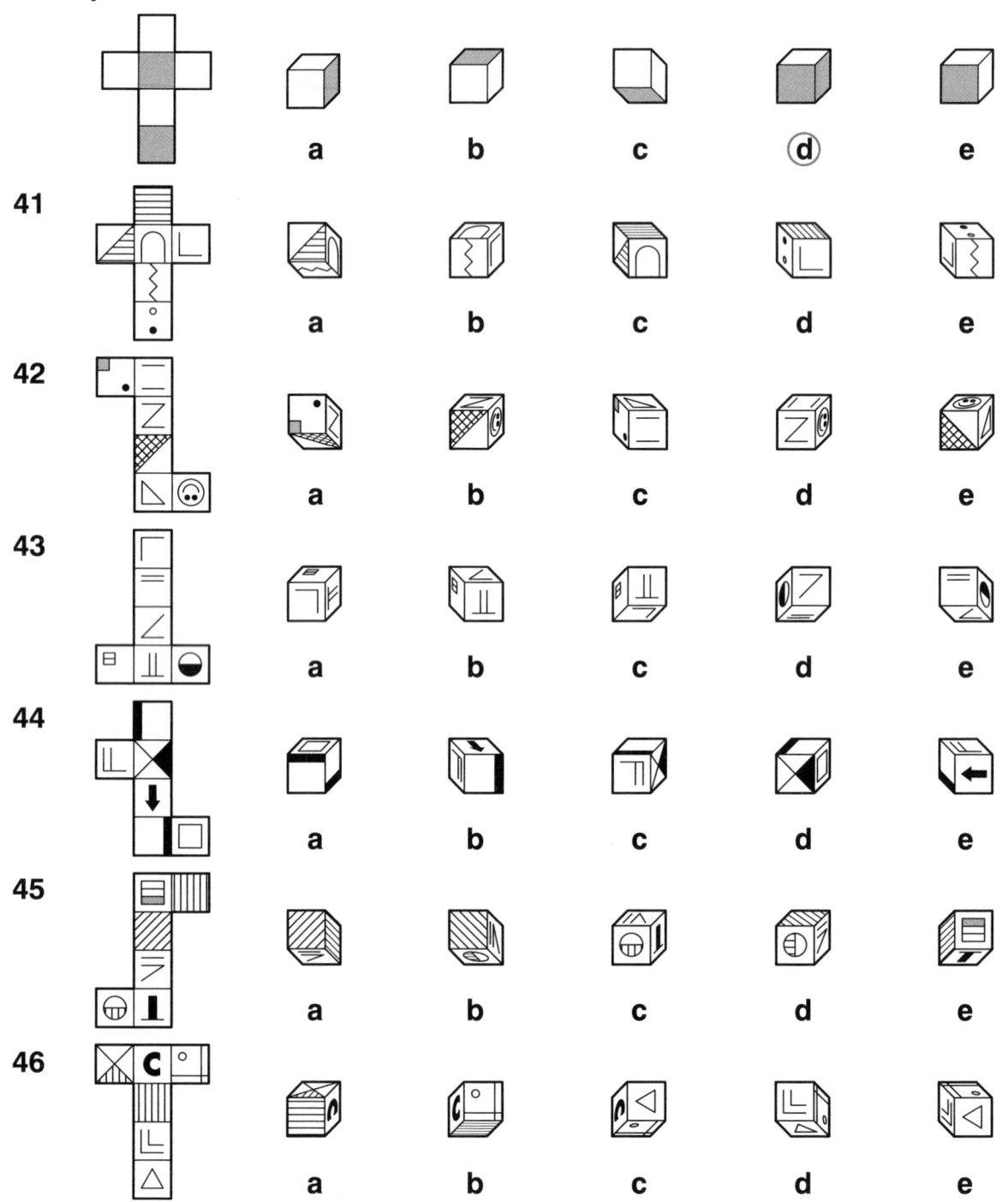

Example

a b c **(d)** e

41

a b c d e

42

a b c d e

43

a b c d e

44

a b c d e

45

a b c d e

46

a b c d e

47

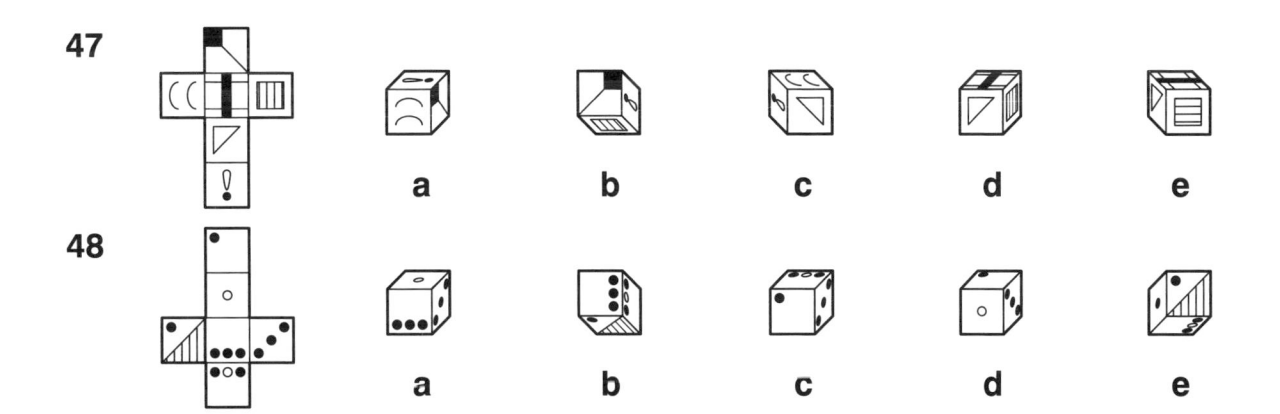

48

Using the given patterns and codes, work out the code that matches the last pattern. Circle the letter.

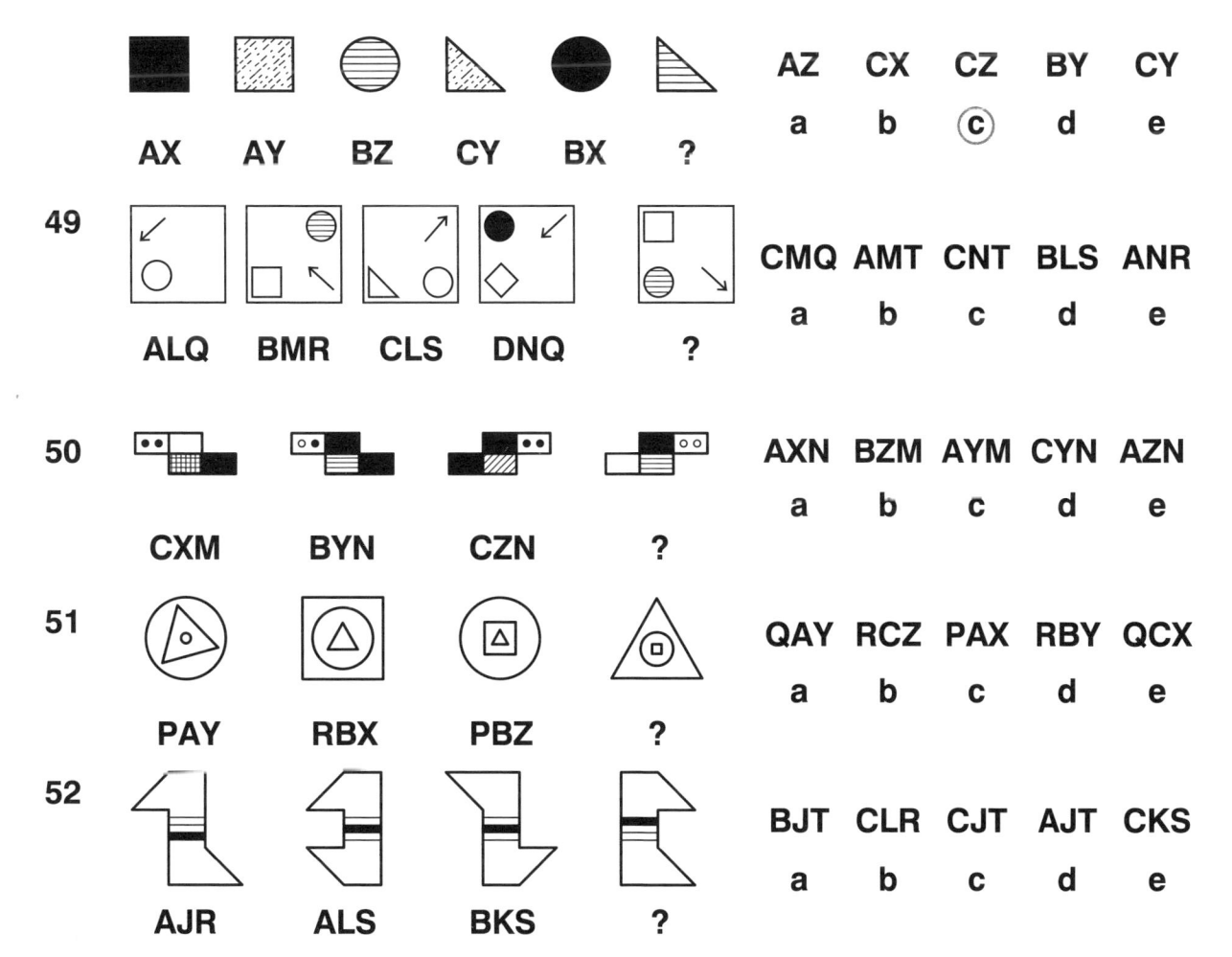

Example

AZ	CX	CZ	BY	CY
a	b	ⓒ	d	e

AX AY BZ CY BX ?

49

CMQ AMT CNT BLS ANR
 a   b   c   d   e

ALQ BMR CLS DNQ ?

50

AXN BZM AYM CYN AZN
 a   b   c   d   e

CXM BYN CZN ?

51

QAY RCZ PAX RBY QCX
 a   b   c   d   e

PAY RBX PBZ ?

52

BJT CLR CJT AJT CKS
 a   b   c   d   e

AJR ALS BKS ?

53 BMX CMY ANY ? BNZ BNX CMZ BMZ CNY
          a   b   c   d   e

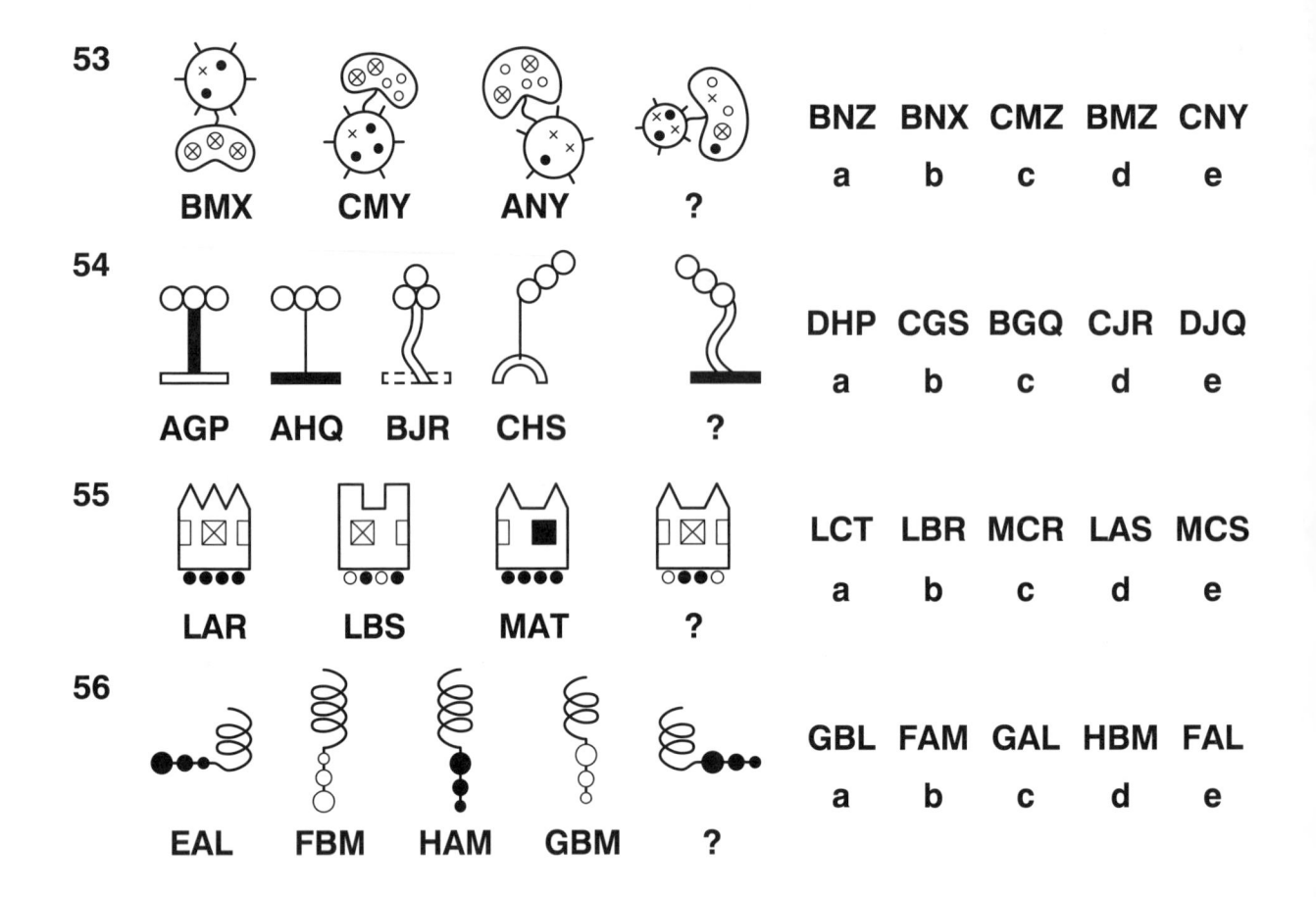

54 AGP AHQ BJR CHS ? DHP CGS BGQ CJR DJQ
          a   b   c   d   e

55 LAR LBS MAT ? LCT LBR MCR LAS MCS
          a   b   c   d   e

56 EAL FBM HAM GBM ? GBL FAM GAL HBM FAL
          a   b   c   d   e

Which pattern on the right is made by combining the two shapes on the left? Circle the letter.

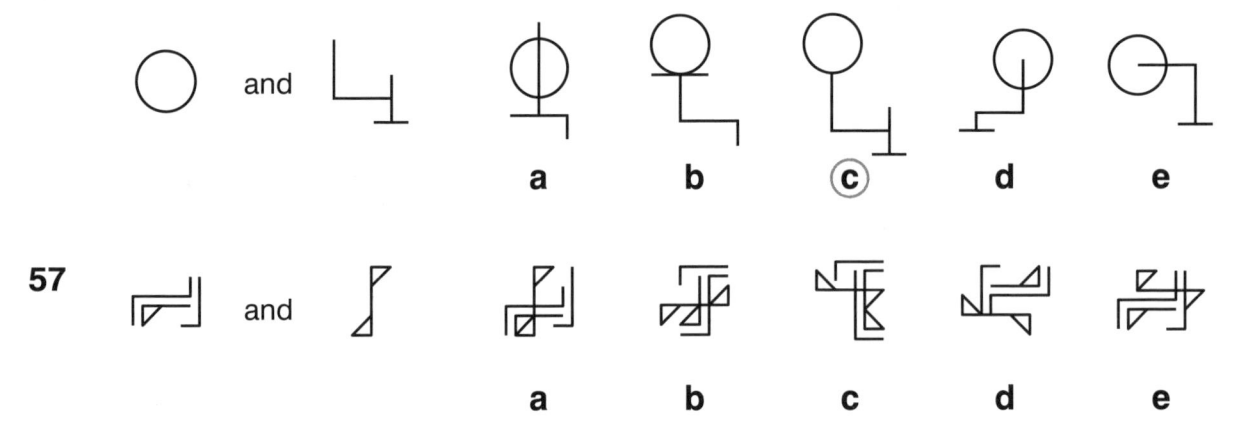

Example

   ○ and ⌐ a b c d e

57 and   a b c d e

58

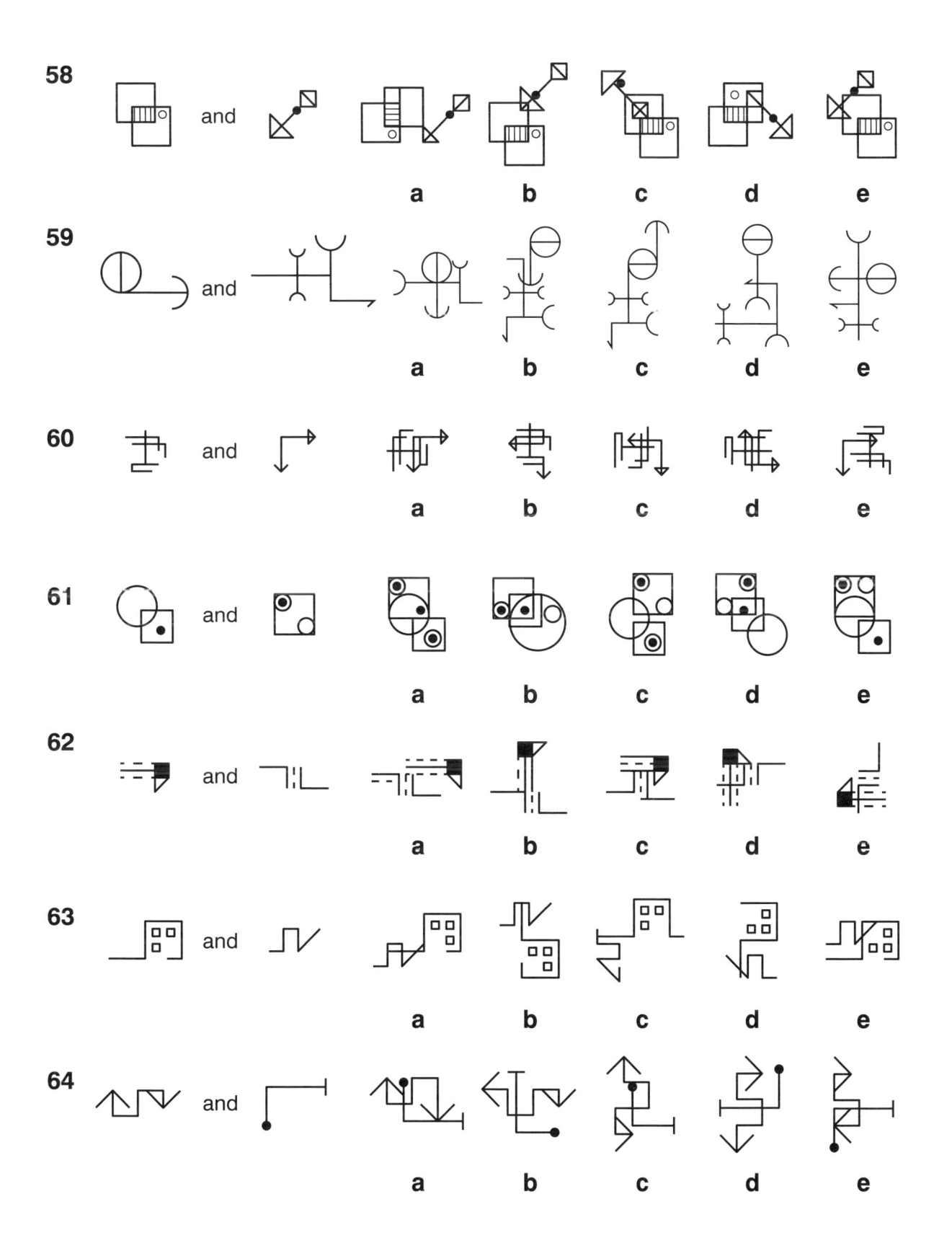

59

60

61

62

63

64

Now go to the Progress Chart ... **49** *... to record your score!* **Total** **64**

Mixed paper 4

Which of the shapes belongs to the group on the left? Circle the letter.

Example

1
2
3
4
5
6
7
8

Which shape or pattern completes the pattern on the left? Circle the letter.

Example

a b (c) d e

9

a b c d e

10

a b c d e

11

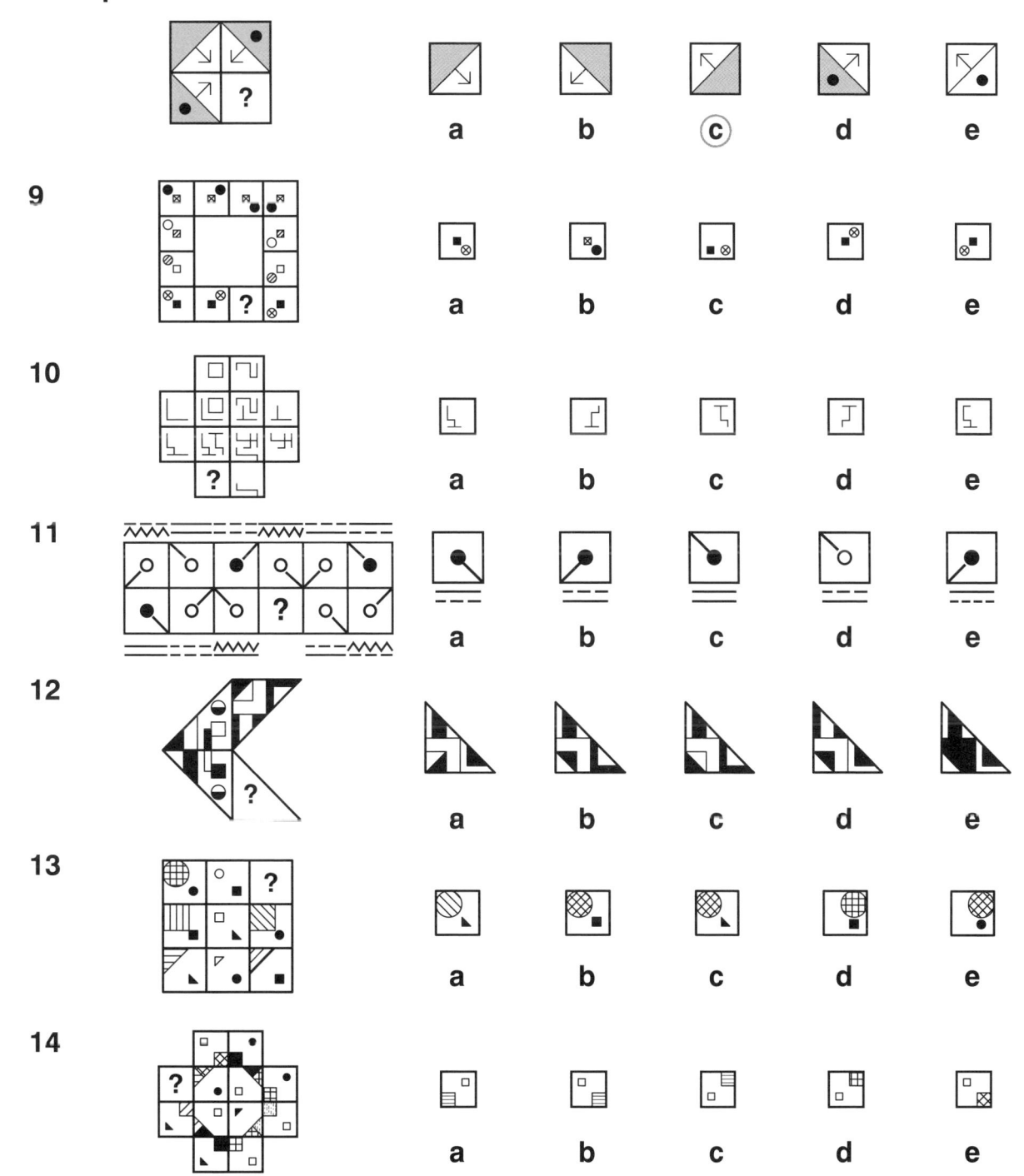

a b c d e

12

a b c d e

13

a b c d e

14

a b c d e

15

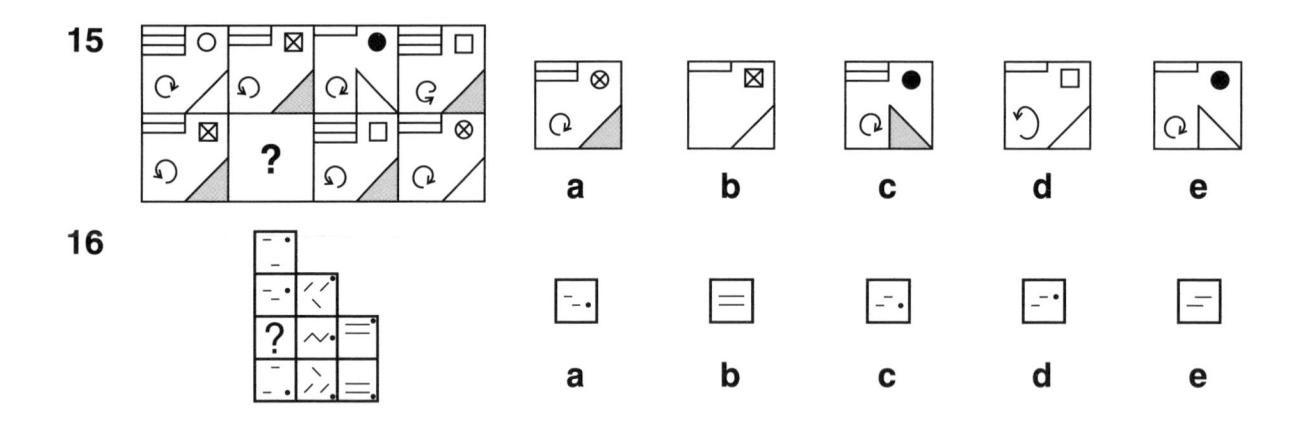

16

Which shape or pattern completes the second pair in the same way as the first pair? Circle the letter.

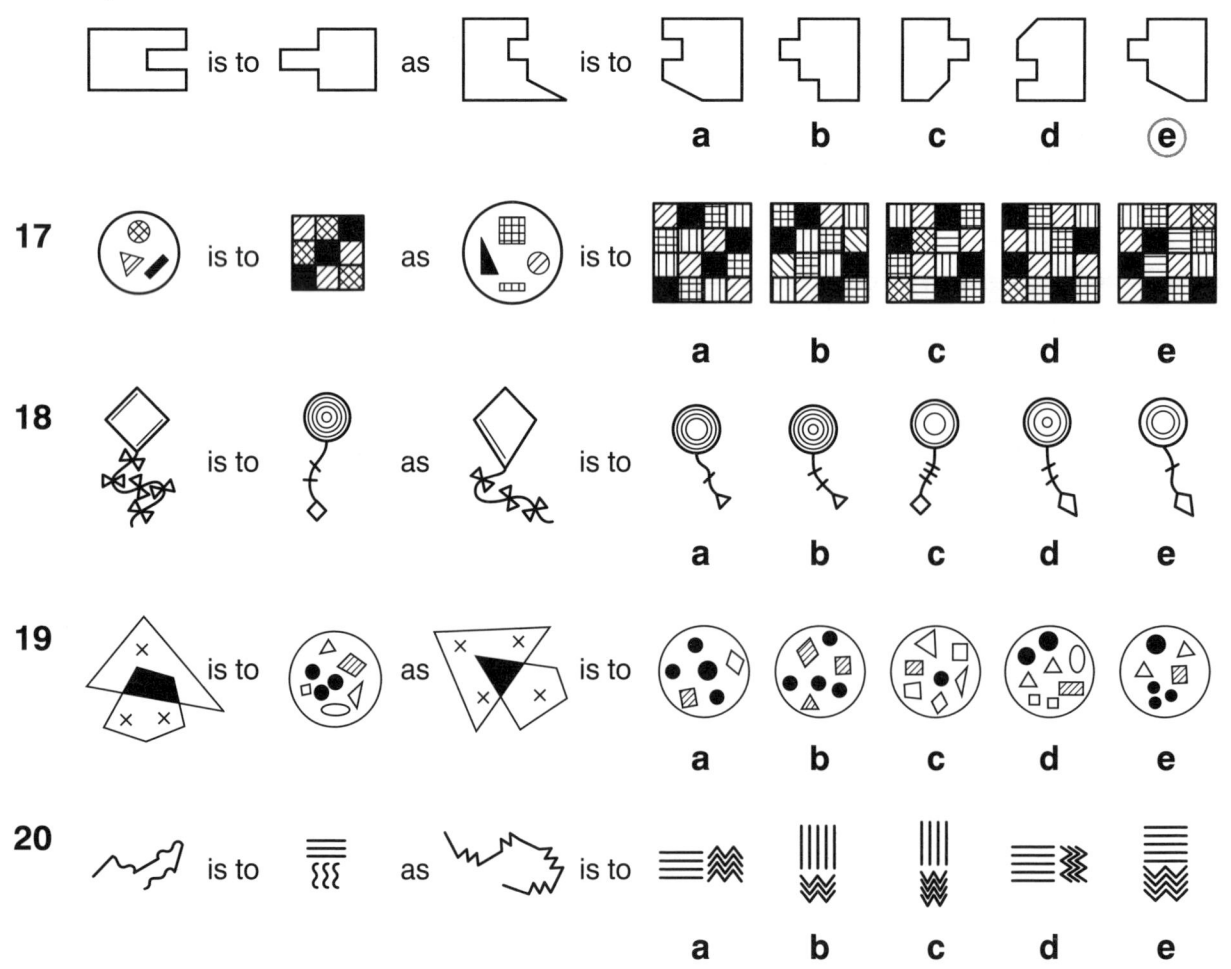

Example

is to … as … is to … a b c d **e**

17 is to … as … is to … a b c d e

18 is to … as … is to … a b c d e

19 is to … as … is to … a b c d e

20 is to … as … is to … a b c d e

21 — **22** — **23** — **24**

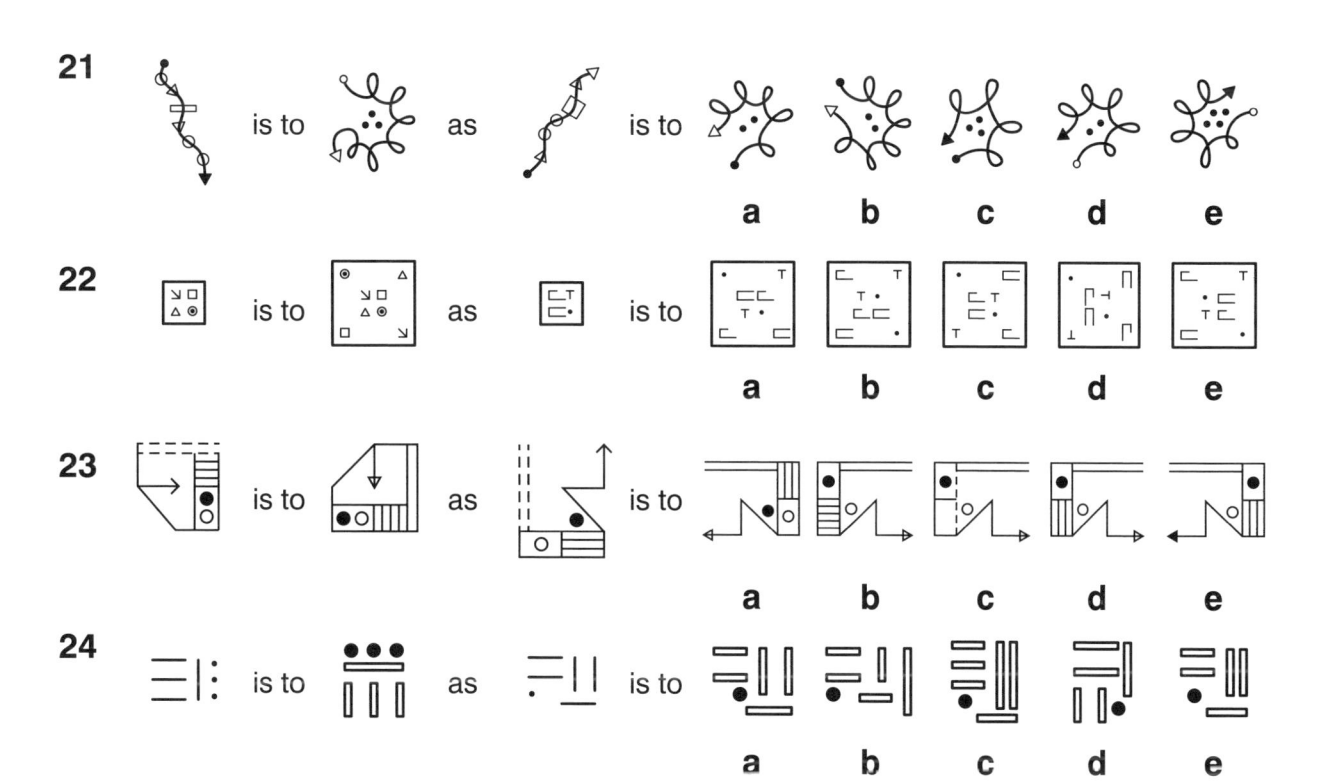

Which shape or pattern is a reflection of the shape on the left? Circle the letter.

Example

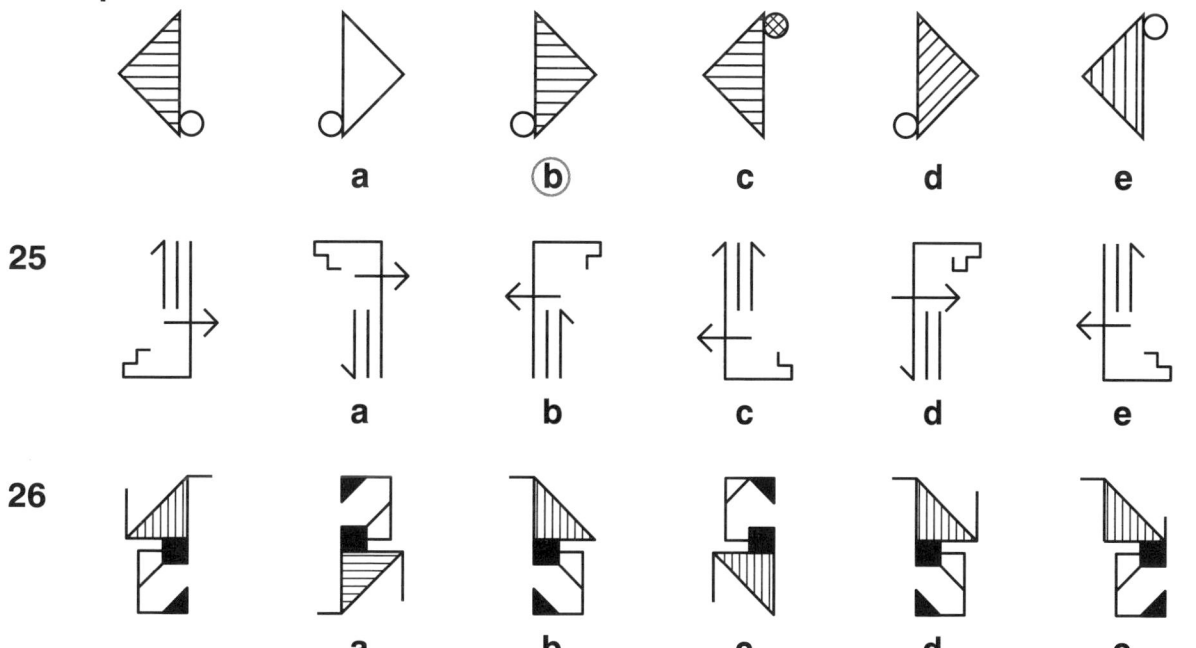

25 — **26**

27

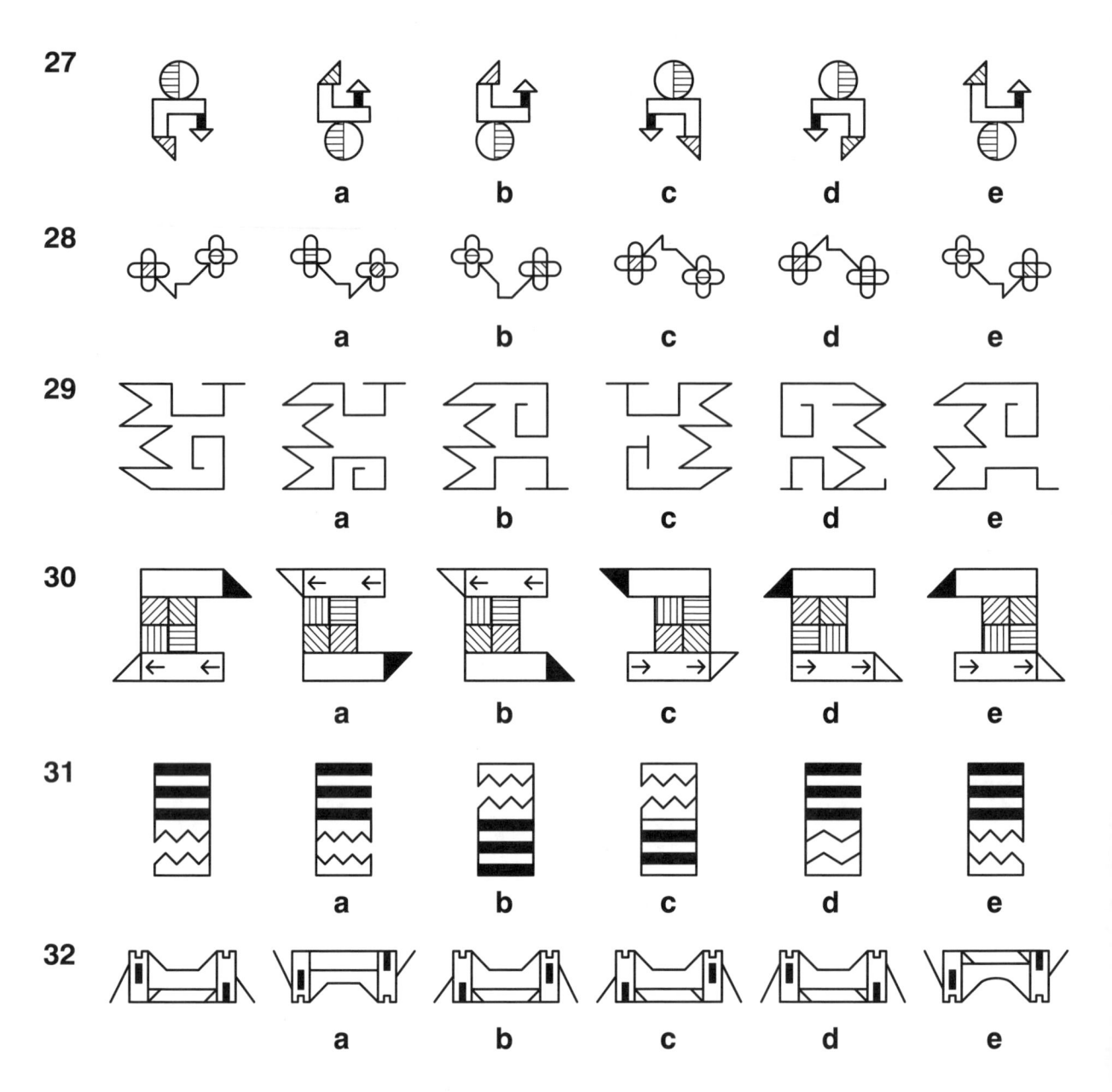

28

29

30

31

32

a b c d e

Which shape or pattern continues or completes the given sequence? Circle the letter.

Example

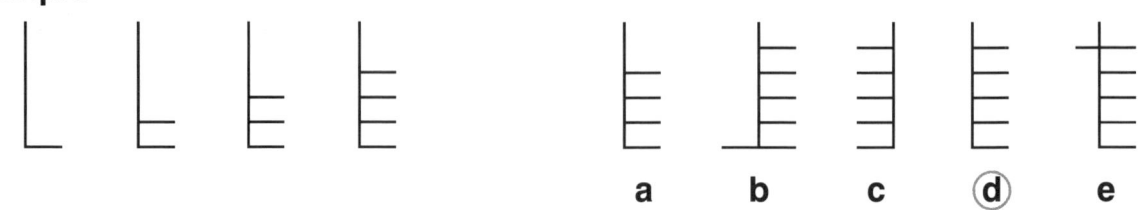

a b c (d) e

33

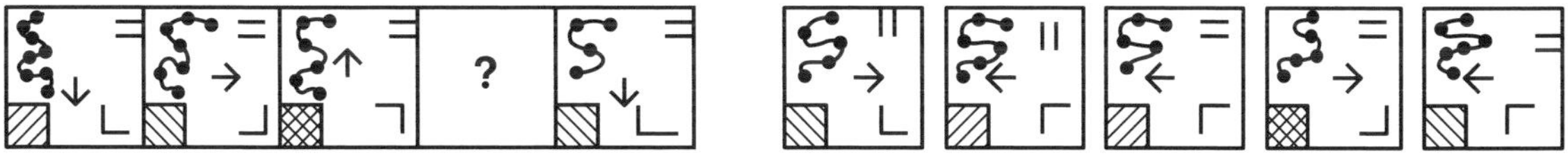

a b c d e

34

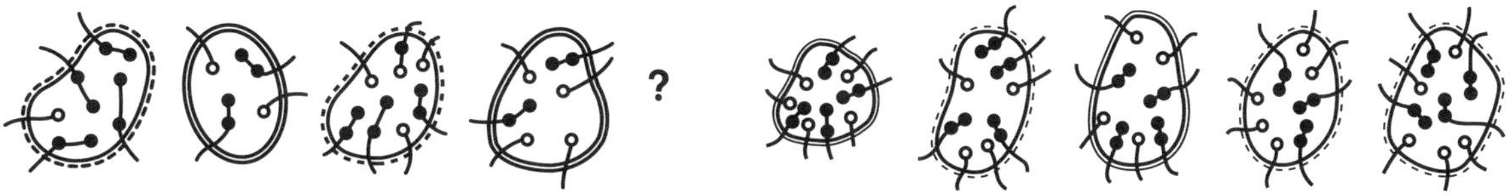

a b c d e

35

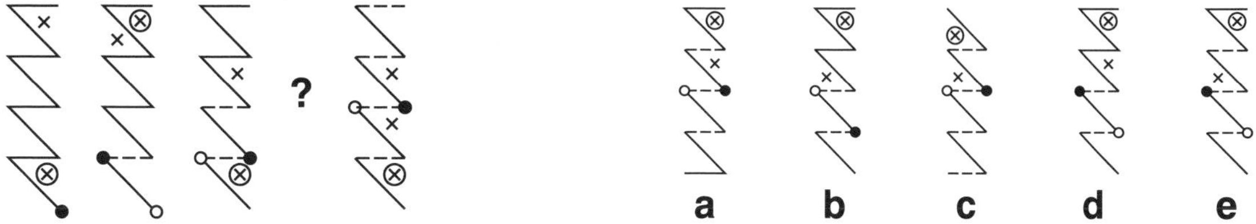

a b c d e

36

a b c d e

37

a b c d e

38

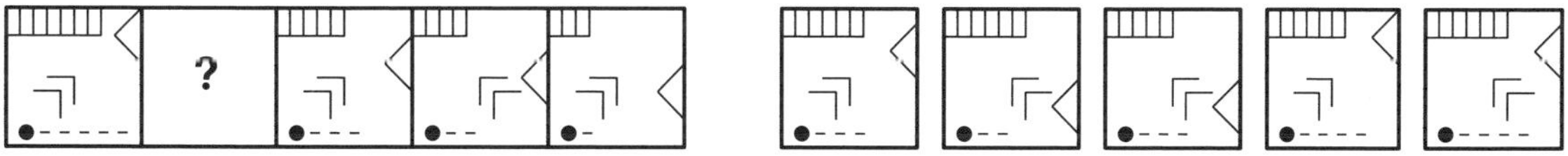

a b c d e

39

a b c d e

40

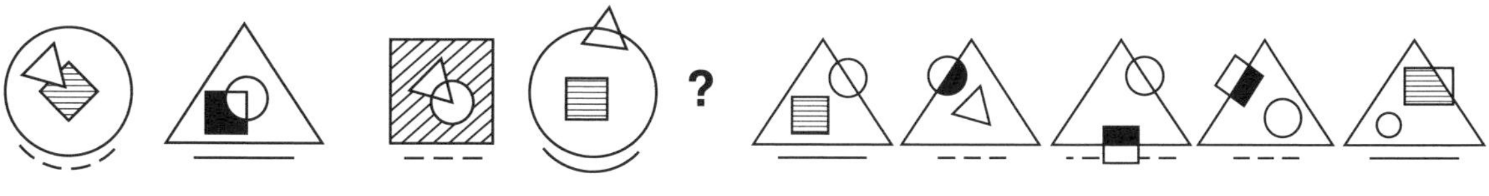

a b c d e

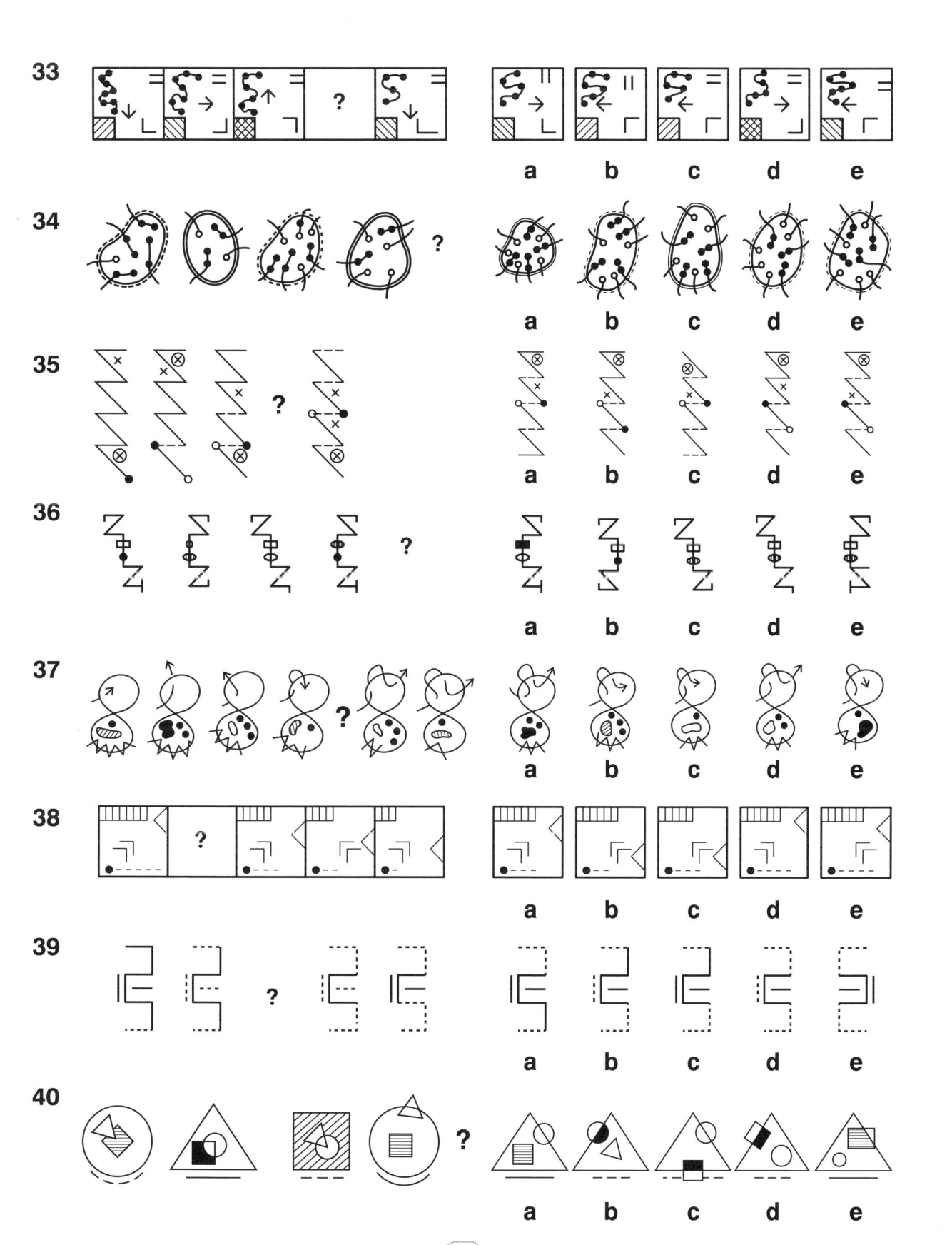

Which cube could not be made from the given net? Circle the letter.

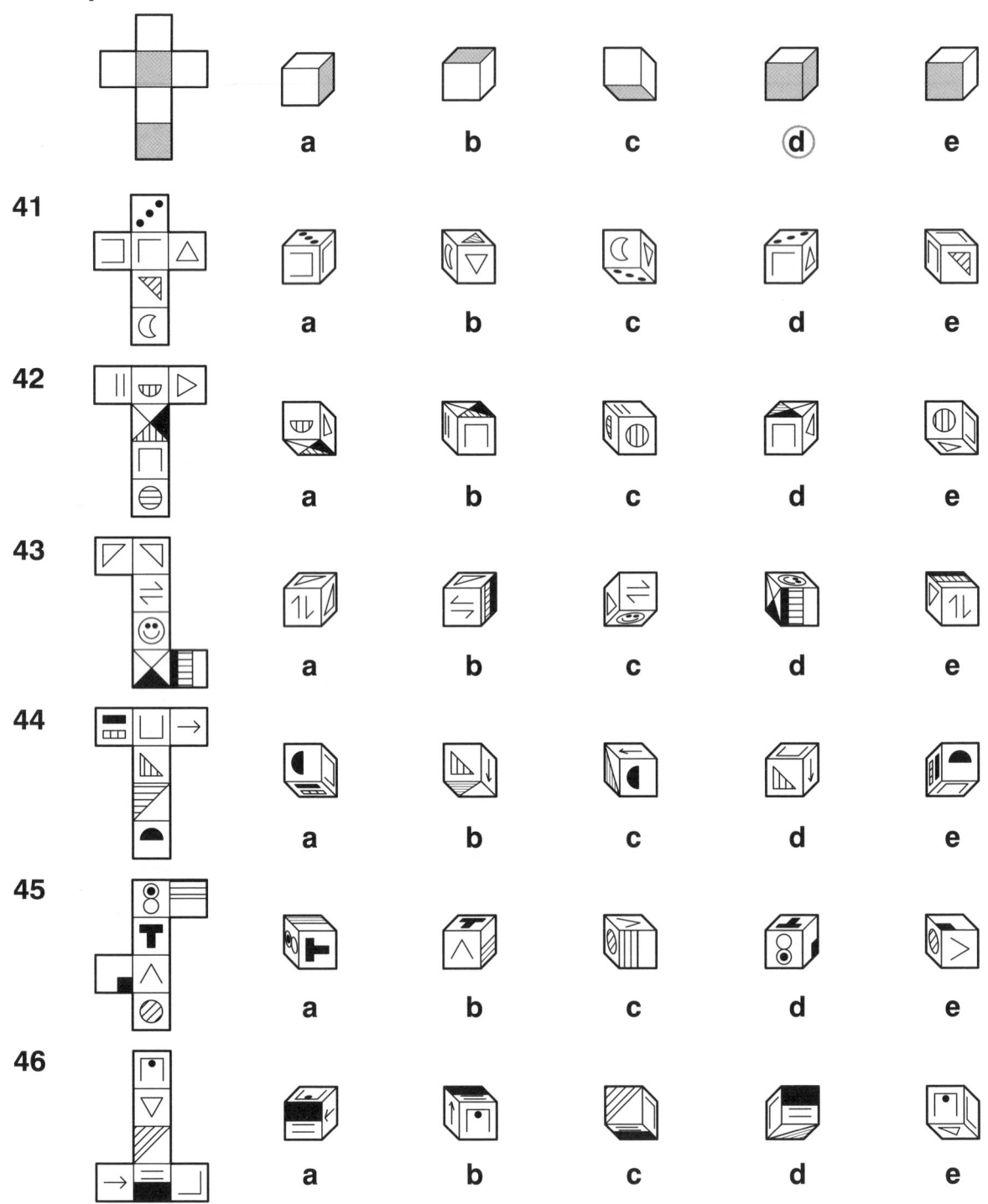

Example

a b c (d) e

41   a b c d e

42   a b c d e

43   a b c d e

44   a b c d e

45   a b c d e

46   a b c d e

47

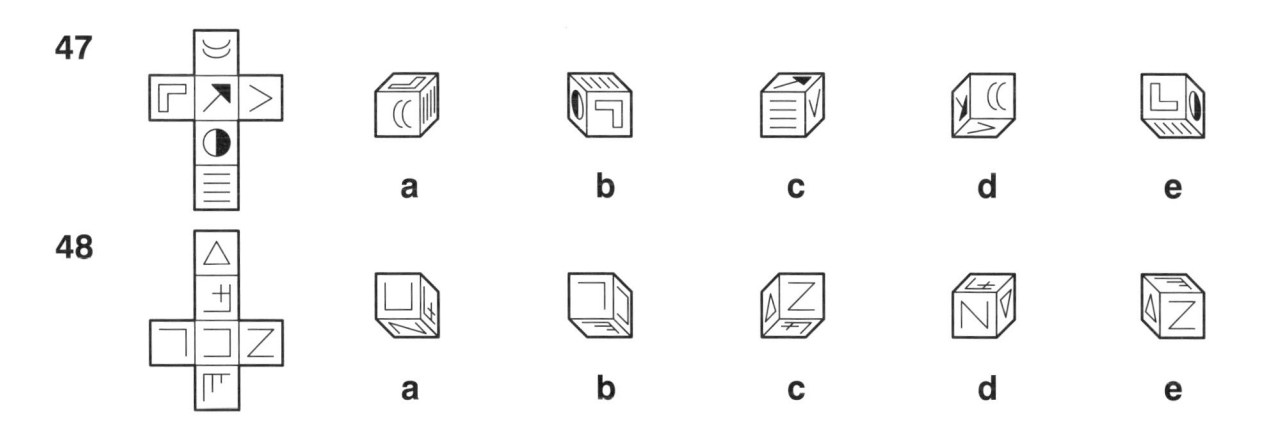

48

Using the given patterns and codes, work out the code that matches the last pattern. Circle the letter.

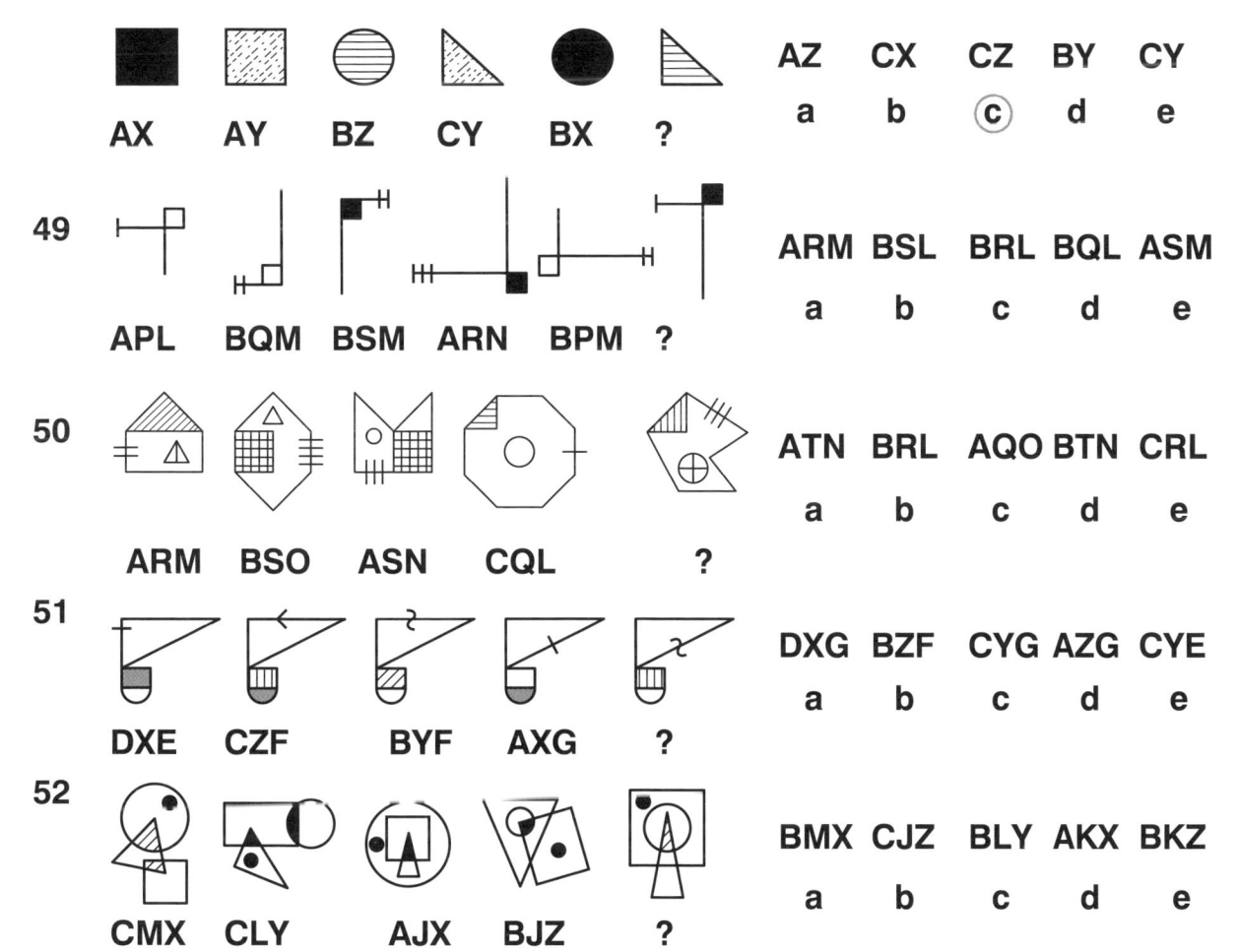

Example

AX   AY   BZ   CY   BX   ?

AZ   CX   CZ   BY   CY
a   b   ⓒ   d   e

49

APL   BQM   BSM   ARN   BPM   ?

ARM   BSL   BRL   BQL   ASM
a   b   c   d   e

50

ARM   BSO   ASN   CQL   ?

ATN   BRL   AQO   BTN   CRL
a   b   c   d   e

51

DXE   CZF   BYF   AXG   ?

DXG   BZF   CYG   AZG   CYE
a   b   c   d   e

52

CMX   CLY   AJX   BJZ   ?

BMX   CJZ   BLY   AKX   BKZ
a   b   c   d   e

53

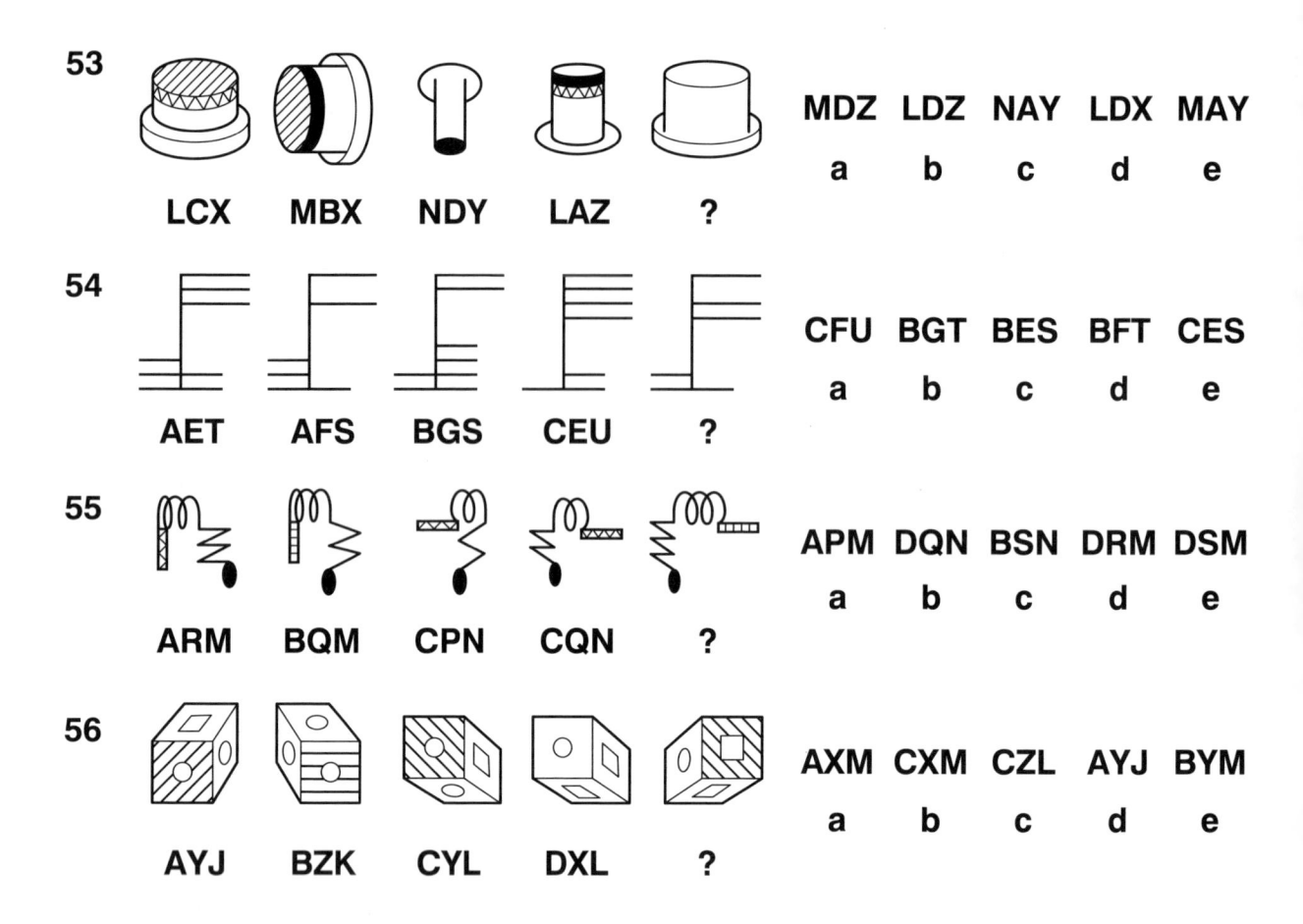

LCX MBX NDY LAZ ?

MDZ LDZ NAY LDX MAY
 a   b   c   d   e

54

AET AFS BGS CEU ?

CFU BGT BES BFT CES
 a   b   c   d   e

55

ARM BQM CPN CQN ?

APM DQN BSN DRM DSM
 a   b   c   d   e

56

AYJ BZK CYL DXL ?

AXM CXM CZL AYJ BYM
 a   b   c   d   e

Which pattern on the right is made by combining the two shapes on the left? Circle the letter.

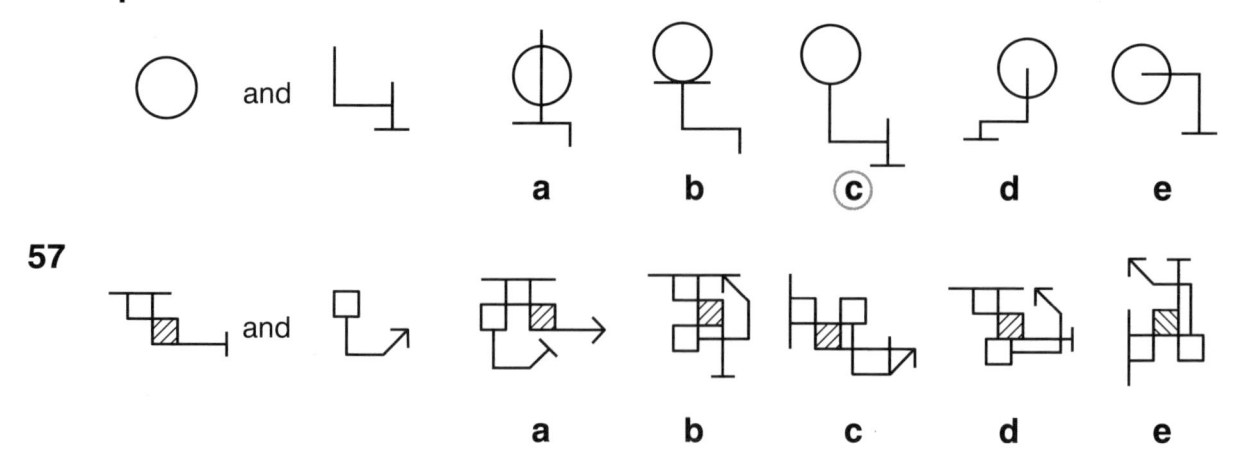

Example

 a   b   (c)   d   e

57

 a   b   c   d   e

58

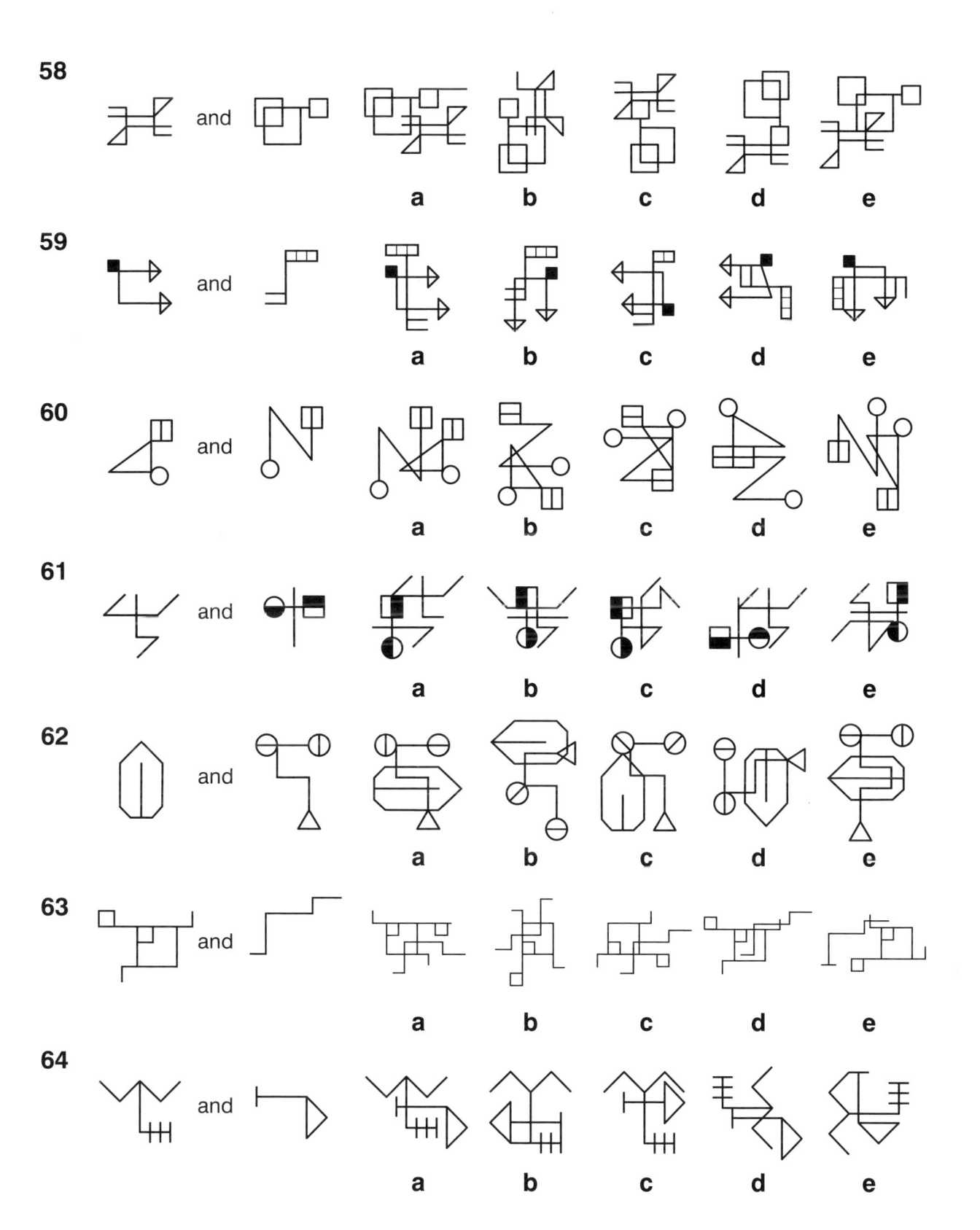

59

60

61

62

63

64